PSYCHOLOGY RESEARCH PROGRESS

INTEGRATING BEHAVIOURAL AND COGNITIVE PSYCHOLOGY

A MODERN CATEGORIZATION THEORETICAL APPROACH

PSYCHOLOGY RESEARCH PROGRESS

Additional books in this series can be found on Nova's website under the Series tab.

Additional e-books in this series can be found on Nova's website under the e-book tab.

PSYCHOLOGY RESEARCH PROGRESS

INTEGRATING BEHAVIOURAL AND COGNITIVE PSYCHOLOGY

A MODERN CATEGORIZATION THEORETICAL APPROACH

DARREN J. EDWARDS, PH.D.

NOVINKA

New York

Library of Congress Cataloging-in-Publication Data

ISBN: 978-1-63463-477-9

Published by Nova Science Publishers, Inc. † New York

CONTENTS

PREFACE

This book has been written for a wide audience, from an undergraduate and layperson looking to explore the history and development of cognitive and behavioural psychology, to experts in the area interested in the integration of modern behavioural and cognitive psychology.

Chapter 1 offers a very basic overview of how psychology developed as a science from its historic philosophical beginnings in ancient Greece to where it is today where cognitive psychology dominates the subject.

Chapter 2 goes on further to explore the rise of behaviourism as psychology entered into the realm of scientific methodology and then explains its fall, with the rise of cognitive psychology and the advent of Chomsky's universal generative grammar, which behaviourism has no answer for.

Chapter 3 follows on from this by explaining the development of Cognitive and Behavioural Therapy (CBT), and how this was the first serious attempt in psychology to integrate cognitive and behavioural theories into a unified model for clinical practice. Chapter 3 also compares and contrasts with another up-and-coming cognitive-behavioural model: Acceptance and Commitment Therapy (ACT) and its Relational Frame Theory (RFT) mechanistic underpinnings. RFT is described in the context of refuting some of Chomsky's most damaging criticisms towards Skinner's (behaviourism) Verbal Behaviour (i.e., universal generative grammar), which to this day has not been adequately refuted by the behavioural community. RFT is offered as a potentially more acceptable and progressive model towards a universally integrated cognitive-behavioural model.

Chapter 4 starts by explaining the basics of cognitive psychology, and the extension of Chomsky's work in the form of categorization. A complete model of cognitive psychology is not given but we include the major components of cognitive discipline: categorization.

Chapters 5, 6, and 7 give specific detailed accounts of three areas within categorization work. Simpler accounts are also provided for those without a mathematical modeling background. Though the intention here is not to intimidate the reader with complex math, it is provided to give the reader an idea as to how complex some of these mathematical models are and what categorization modelers are focusing on today.

Chapter 8 ends the book by bringing together many elements of categorization theories and behavioural theories to demonstrate great commonalities between these subjects and the nature of some of the dichotomy in the language used when describing these. Several examples are provided, which indicate that through a more moderate and less radical perspective of these two subjects, they are completely compatible and cognitive and behavioural words can be used interchangeably. As a final thought, some explanation is then given which explains the advantages of further integrative work in the future. I hope this book enlightens your thinking about the many similarities between cognitive and behavioural psychology.

Chapter 1

A HISTORICAL VIEW: THE FIRST AGE OF PSYCHOLOGY; STRUCTURALISM, FUNCTIONALISM AND PSYCHOANALYSIS

The etymology of the word 'psychology', translates from Latin, "the study of the soul", and was first referenced in 1694 by the Dutch Physician, Steven Blankaart, who defined the difference between the studies of anatomy and psychology. He stated, "Anatomy, which treats the body, and Psychology which treats the soul". References to what is considered today as psychology, however, can be traced back to Classical Greece, in philosophy from iconic philosophers such as Thales, Plato, and Aristotle (e.g., in his De Anima treatise). An example of this is in the 4th century BC, when Hippocrates theorized that mental disorders were physical, rather than divine in nature.

Many centuries later, psychology was finally to enter the realm of the scientific method, and in 1879, Wilhelm Wundt founded Structuralism. This was influenced by the current philosophical theories at that time, about ascertaining truth and knowledge, with the rise of logical positivism, which sought objective verification, and later became known as empirical investigation (i.e., to seek knowledge through empirical evidence). Structuralism of psychology was motivated by the physical sciences, such as how Chemists would break down the elements and analyze the structural components of Chemistry, where, so to, it was believed that mental processes could be broken down and analyzed in a similar fashion. An example of this is when Edward Titchener suggested that consciousness should be examined by trained introspection, and broken down into this component.

In the early 20th Century, a new movement was beginning, called functionalism, which opposed the prevailing structuralism thought to have originated with William James. These ideas, suggested that beliefs, sensations such as pain, desires etc., are constituted only by their function. For example, the individual has causal relations with sensory inputs, other mental states, and behavioural outputs.

Another emergent field of psychology called psychoanalysis was developing in the late 19th century with Josef Breuer, who mentored Sigmund Freud. Psychoanalysis, as it emerged through the Victorian era, with the prevailing community values of Victorian morality such as sexual restraint and low tolerance to crime, could have influenced its development. This clinical theory was developed to deal with the internal conflict of such oppressive morality, such as sexual repression, desires, etc., with various introspective methods used, such as free association. However, these theories were later heavily criticized by Karl Popper and psychologist, Hans Eysenck, for being unscientific (e.g., lacking falsifiability). A new culture in psychology was beginning to emerge, where scientific methodology was taking precedence over subjective experience and philosophy.

From the early 20th Century to the present, psychology has exploded with new psychological theories and approaches to understanding mental processes and behaviour. Some of these include behaviourism, cognitive psychology, social psychology, developmental psychology, and neuroscience. The scope of this book only allows for focus to be placed on cognitive and behavioural psychology, however, it should be mentioned that many of the other disciplines have overlaps with the current dominant theory of today (cognitive psychology), such as Piaget's cognitive development for developmental psychology and many FMRI brain scanning experiments on memory and attention, etc., for neuroscience. The focus of this book is specifically the integration and analysis of cognitive and behavioural psychology.

So, to start with, by the 1950s behaviourism grew as the dominant theory of psychology and with it brought scientific rigor of testable cause and effect, (which there was a growing appetite for). Behaviourism utilized experiments based on highly controlled variables and outcomes, based on reinforcing and punishing certain behaviours to lead to behavioural reshaping. This is explained in much greater depth in the next Chapter, but for now as a taste, the reader should be aware that these experiments were highly successful but most probably overly focused on just behaviour. This 'over-focus' on behaviour and rejection of any other elements led to behaviourism's downfall. Chomsky's (one of the very early cognitive psychologists) work (a rebuke of Skinner's

Verbal Behaviour) more or less destroyed behaviourism in one blow, as it attacked Skinner's (the leading behaviourist at the time) approach to explaining verbal behaviour, which used an overly rigid behavioural model of reinforcement. Skinner, using his very constricted model of direct reinforcement as a requirement for all verbal behaviour, prevented him from answering tough questions about how humans are able to generate language almost in an infinite amount of ways and with the same basic underlying grammar in every part of the world (even extremely remote regions), which was impossible to directly teach and reinforce.

Chomsky's cognitive linguistics relied on hardwired information in the brain presumably encoded by DNA, which allowed universal grammar to be accounted for. The ability to cognitively infer information was an important aspect to the infinite generation of language from a finite set of words. Behaviourism, to this day, still has not provided an adequate account for this. Therefore, one of the goals of this book is to peel back some of the constrictive narrow-minded thinking from both sides of subject radicalists (cognitive and behavioural) and to explain and offer some integration, which can account for Chomsky's work and far beyond.

As mentioned, today, the dominant theory in psychology is cognitive psychology, and the term 'cognitive science', was coined in 1967 by Ulric Neisser, who used this to mean all processes by which the sensory input is transformed, reduced, elaborated, stored, recovered, and used. Neisser (1967) refers to people as being dynamic information-processing systems whereby a description of their mental operations can be given in computational terms. The origins of ideas in cognitive psychology, such as the computational theory of mind, can be traced back to Descartes (17th century) and continued with Alan Turing (1940s-1950s) and Claude Shannon's (1948) information theory. This basic foundation of cognitive psychology allowed the development of more thorough attempts to understand how we process and organize information in terms of information processing, and has led to the development of the complex categorization theories that we have today (these will be fully explored in Chapters 4, 5, 6 and 7).

Today in cognitive psychology, there are very complex mathematical descriptions about how information is organized in terms of spontaneous (e.g., the simplicity model, Pothos & Chater, 2002) and supervised categorization (e.g., the generalized context model, Nosofsky; 1986), which uses information theory and cognition. These models provide us with a rich range of predictions about how information can be organized when we have no past knowledge of it (spontaneous), and how information is organized when there is an external agent guiding classification (supervised). We also have evidence as to how relative properties can affect classification decisions, which are abstract properties that do not depend on the physical appearance of a stimulus that the most spontaneous and supervised models depend on. This is through the work carried out on shared properties in analogical mapping and also categorization models such as the relative judgment model and recent work on absolute vs. relational properties in categorization (Edwards, Perlaman & Pothos, 2012).

Finally, to reiterate, the focus of this book is to explore the history of cognitive and behavioural psychology and to bring about some new developing trends in how these historical rivals are beginning to emerge and integrate at a much needed theoretical level.

Chapter 2

The Rise and Fall of Behaviourism; Heralding Chomsky and Cognitive Psychology

The Second Age of Psychology and First Wave of Behaviourism; B.F. Skinner, and the Rise of Radical Behaviourism

The rise of behaviourism began when John Watson pioneered the area of study and published, "Psychology as the behaviourist views it" in 1913. His interest in the field developed with the classic Little Albert study. This was a case study, which demonstrated that at baseline, Little Albert (a very young child) demonstrated no fear when presented with a white rat. However, in another situation when a loud noise was made every time Little Albert reached out for the rat, he then became distressed. In a later condition, Little Albert would become distressed with the presence of the rat even when there was no loud noise present. In yet another condition, Little Albert displayed distress even when there was a brown rabbit, suggesting that the fear response had transferred to all furry animals.

At about the same time, Ivan Pavlov, a Russian psychologist became famous for his 'conditioned reflex' (1901), also referred to as Pavlovian conditioning or classical conditioning. This conditioning occurs when a conditioned stimulus (CS) is paired with an unconditioned stimulus (US). To demonstrate this, in experiment, Pavlov (1927) observed that placing meat powder (the unconditioned stimuli; US) next to a dog's mouth resulted in an unconditioned response (UR) in the form of the dog salivating. When Pavlov then paired the meat powder with the sound of a bell, then the bell became the conditioned stimuli (CS) resulting in the conditioned response (CR) of salivation, so that even when the meat powder was removed, and the bell was sounded the dog would still salivate.

Operant Conditioning

The next major form of behaviourism, and an evolution from classical conditioning was B. F. Skinner's radical behaviourism (1974). Radical behaviourism seeks to understand behaviour as a function of environmental histories and reinforcing consequences. Using functional analysis, specific techniques of Applied Behavioural Analysis are used to understand and treat clinical and non-clinical patients such as in autism spectrum disorders (e.g., Dillenburger & Keenan, M. 2009).

Burrhus Frederic Skinner adopted less extreme views than Watson, and accepted that there was a mind, but believed that it was more sensible to study the outputs of the mind, i.e., behaviour, rather than using introspection. The major difference between a classical and an operant condition is that a classical condition involves developing associations between events, whereas an operant condition involves learning from the consequences of the individual's behaviour. The first researcher to study learning by consequence (Skinner coined the term operant conditioning many years later), was Edward Thorndike.

Skinner's theory of operant conditioning was based on that of Thorndike (1905), who studied the learning of animals using a puzzle box to propose the theory of 'law and effect'. Thorndike (1898) studied animals in an experiment he called the puzzle box, to empirically test the laws of learning. To do this, he placed a cat in the puzzle box, which was then encouraged to escape and reach fish outside of the box. Thorndike would time how long it would take the cat to get at the fish. Eventually, the cat would stumble across a level that would open the box and allow the cat to get at the fish. The cat was then put back into the box with same experiment. This time, Thorndike observed a reduction in how long it would take the cat to press the level. Again, on several more successions of this basic experiment the cat would become faster and faster at pressing the lever. From this simple observation, Thorndike put forward a theory called the 'law and effect', which stated that any behaviour that led to a pleasant outcome was more likely to be repeated, and any behaviour that led to unpleasant consequences would likely be stopped. This would later become the basis of Skinners operant conditioning.

Skinner introduced a new term into 'law and effect', which was called 'reinforcement'. The basis of operant conditioning was that behaviour that was reinforced tended to be repeated (i.e., strengthened), whilst behaviour that was not reinforced tended to die-out or be extinguished (i.e., weakened). Skinner (1948) used a similar experiment, which Thorndike used (the puzzle box), but called it the 'skinner box'. The term 'operant conditioning' was coined by Skinner (Skinner, 1938) to mean the changing of behaviour by the use of reinforcement. He identified three types of operants; 1) A neutral operant, which neither increased nor decreased the tendency of behaviour; 2) Reinforces, which increase the tendency of a behaviour (these can be positive or negative). 3) Punishers, which decrease the tendency for behaviour. A theory that developed from operant conditioning is 'behaviour modification', which comprises changes in the environmental events that are related to a person's behaviour, for example reinforcing desirable behaviour and punishing undesirable ones.

One of Skinner's most important pieces was his work on verbal behaviourism (Skinner, 1957) called *Verbal Behaviour,* which used operant reinforcement in the area of linguistics. In this work (and follow up work) he describes a four-term contingency model; motivating operation; discriminative stimulus; response and reinforcement, and also six basic verbal operants; mand, tact, audience relation, echoic, textual and intraverbal. A mand is described as a verbal behaviour that motivates operations through satiation or deprivation reinforces, and can be a command, a request, etc. A nonverbal version of a mand could be a knock on the door, where someone is requesting to enter a room. Skinner also described other behaviours that could be controlled through verbal stimuli such as textual, which was behaviour controlled through reading or writing (e.g., a written request to open the door). Another was echoic, which is the repetition of verbal stimuli, such as when a teacher asks a child to repeat the word 'parsimonious', and the teacher reinforces this behaviour by saying 'correct'. Tacts are nonverbal reinforcements such as those produced by the physical environment, where the individual may describe her surroundings, such as 'it is hot today', and someone may say 'that's correct'. Intraverbals are verbal behaviours under the control of other verbal behaviour, such as a mother saying 'well done' to a child who says she had an A in an exam. An autoclitic is where the reinforcer is the own persons verbal behaviour, such as a child saying 'I am sick' and the parent responding to help. Audience reinforcement is where the audience may be positive or negative, and certain behaviour can become more or less likely given the level of positive or negative reinforcements responded to from the audience, such as from friends, family, and colleagues.

These techniques have become very useful in terms of behaviour shaping (or behaviour modification) efforts in therapy, especially in clinical disorders such as autism when utilizing applied behavioural analysis (e.g., Maurice, Green, & Luce, 1996). Applied Behavioural Analysis (ABA) uses functional analysis (described in detail in Chapter 3) and explores specific behaviours, which need to be shaped or modified in frequency through reinforcement. Reinforces can be positive, e.g., praising good behaviour, negative, e.g., punishing bad behaviour to lead to the reduction in frequency or extinction for bad behaviour and positive reinforcements to increase good behaviour. In situations such as autism, many of the basic verbal operants are used to reinforce behaviour modification, since verbal language and behaviour are often highly related. ABA may be one of the most successful forms of therapy for behavioural change, grounded in behaviourism, which is obviously a theory that should not be discounted.

THE RISE OF CHOMSKY AND THE THIRD AGE OF PSYCHOLOGY; COGNITIVE PSYCHOLOGY

Noam Chomsky's father, William Chomsky, was a famous Hebrew linguist, and Chomsky read his father's work from an early age; *David Kimhi's Hebrew Grammar*, a study of thirteenth-century Hebrew Grammar. Later, at the age of sixteen he began his undergraduate studies at the University of Pennsylvania where he would meet Zellig Harris, a Bloomfieldian linguist. During this meeting, Chomsky read one of Harris's manuscripts called 'Methods in Structural Linguistics' (1951), which first introduced him to formal theoretical linguistics.

Further to this, during Chomsky's masters, he was deeply influenced by Harris's work, and for his thesis; *The Morphophonemics of Modern Hebrew* in 1951, he developed the idea of 'simplicity' for grammars, to sort out the linguistically significant generalizations. In this, he constructed a system of rules for generating the phonetic forms of sentences, and developed a system of recursive rules for describing the form and structure of sentences. From there, Chomsky won a one-year junior fellowship at Harvard, and continued developing his linguistic theory using a non-taxonomic approach based on mathematical formalism. This marked his break from the Bloomfieldian taxonomic structuralist approach of linguistic analysis, and he then wrote his ideas in an oeuvre; *The Logical Structure of Linguistic Theory* (*LSLT*). Later, in 1955, Chomsky went to MIT's Research Laboratory of Electronics and submitted the 9th Chapter of LSLT to gain his Ph.D. from the University of Pennsylvania, but it took another 18 years before the LSLT became published.

LSLT was finally published in 1956, as a shorter version with the title; *Syntactic Structures*. The book attempted to create a formalized theory of linguistic structures and he referred to this fundamental concern as the problem of justification of grammars. There he described a grammar of language L as a theory of L as well as a device that generates all of the grammatical sequences of L and none of the ungrammatical ones. He also compared a finite corpus of utterances of a particular language to 'observations' and grammatical rules to 'laws', which are stated in terms of 'hypothetical constructs' such as phonemes, phrases, etc. Chomsky pointed out that criteria for the 'justification of grammars' are external conditions of adequacy, conditions of generality and simplicity. In order to choose the best grammar for a particular corpus of text, he explained there is an 'evaluation procedure', which chooses the best grammar given a set of criteria; a 'discovery procedure', which is supposed to automatically produce the correct grammar; and a 'decision procedure', which is supposed to automatically choose the best grammar for a language from a set of competing grammars.

Another point that Chomsky raised was the fundamental aim of linguistic analysis of a language L; to separate the grammatical sequences of sentences of L and ungrammatical sequences, which are not sentences of L, and to study the grammatical sequences. There are three ways in which to determine whether a sentence is grammatically correct; its inclusion in a corpus, it being meaningful, and it being statistically probable. To illustrate this point he used the meaningless sentence, 'Colorless green ideas sleep furiously'. In conclusion, Chomsky maintained that grammar is autonomous and independent of meaning and can be statistically improbable to be included in a corpus. Finally, in the book *synaptic structures*, Chomsky attempted to figure out what sort of device or model was required to account for a set of grammatical utterances. He first discussed finite state grammar, which is a theoretic communication model based on the conception of language as a Markov process. He then later discussed a phase structure grammar, which is a model based on immediate constituent analysis. He concluded that these were both inadequate for linguistic description and solution and proposed his own formal theory of syntax called transformational generative grammar (TGG), which combined both phrase structure and grammatical transformations.

The TGG has a tripartite arrangement of; 1) phrase structure rules; 2) transformational rules; and 3) morphophonemic rules. The phase structure rules are used for the expansion of grammatical categories and substitution, which yield a string of morphemes. A transformational rule operates on a given string and with a given constituent structure and converts the string into a new string with a newly derived constituent structure. There are two kinds of transformational rules: obligatory and optional. Obligatory transformations applied to terminal strings produce the kernel of the language, which are simple declarative sentences. Optional transformations are used to create more complex sentences such as morphophonemic rules converting a string of words into a string of phonemes.

The Impact of Chomsky on Behavioural Psychology and Some Final Thoughts on an Unresolved Issue

One of the reasons that behaviourism lost favor with mainstream psychology in the 1960s was because of the rise of Chomsky's transformational generative language (TGG). Chomsky believed that many aspects of language were innate and not learned, as Skinner had previously suggested. For this he developed his Universal Grammar theory, which proposes that as language syntactic structures are hardwired, such as verbs and nouns, and will always be present in all languages. Chomsky also challenged structural linguistics, which proposed that language should be observed as a static set of interconnected units through his transformational grammar (or generative grammar). Chomsky defined, through transformational grammar, two distinct types of grammatical structure: deep and surface structure. Deep structure was thought to be core semantic relations mapped onto the surface structure of phonological form. Through this it can be determined that although the phonological form (e.g., specific words for objects) can be learned and reinforced, the deeper grammatical structure is hardwired.

According to Chomsky, language was constructed through a limited set of hardwired rules known as universal grammar. He also suggested that there was a language acquisition device, which allowed children the innate ability to develop language. As mentioned, in 1957, Chomsky published his first book called Syntactic Structures, which laid out the ideas of transformational grammar.

Chomsky used the word 'generate' to explain that through his transformational generative grammar model, a finite amount of words can potentially generate an infinite amount of sentences (such as the example of a nonsense sentence, which was grammatically correct; 'colorless green ideas sleep furiously). This was used as evidence to debunk Skinner's verbal behaviourism and behaviourism in general. Because sentences can be generated in an infinite amount of ways as described by Chomsky, then direct learning (as Skinner suggested) does not seem applicable or at least is not a complete model for language generation. However, reinforcement clearly does have an impact on the types of specific words generated and the number or words to describe a concept, (which is accounted for by Chomsky). An example of this is when in 1940 Benjamin Whorf, through his hypothesis of linguistic relativity, described how Eskimos had several words for snow, which reflected their view of the world. So, the concept of snow having different types and descriptions would have been reinforced in the Eskimo children, where they might not have been in children from other parts of the world. Given this, reinforcement obviously does shape conceptual understanding but does not explain the generativity of language in the framework that Sinner described, therefore a more complete model of behavioural psychology would need to account for these, which may require the need to include a cognitive inference component. In later Chapters, such as 3 and 8, a behavioural model (Relational Frame Theory; RFT), will be presented, which accounts for this inference in a behavioural model. In such a framework, Chomsky's criticism of behaviourism is reduced to the hard-wired component of grammar vs. pure reinforcement learning, i.e., the generative problem is greatly reduced or completely removed. Through inferring meaning rather than direct learning, then a complex array of language generativity could be enabled. For example, learning directly the meaning of the word 'light' in one situation could be inferred in another situation, hence infinite sentence generation could be achieved with a finite set of directly learned words.

Modern Cognitive-Behavioural Models

In the 1960s and 70s new theories were beginning to emerge, which began to integrate behavioural and cognitive psychology. Albert Bandura (1977), in his social learning theory suggested that behaviour could be learned from the environment through observational learning. Bandura believed that humans are active information processors and think about the relationship between their behaviour and its consequences. He claimed that observational learning could not occur without cognitive processes. In his theory, individuals who are observed are models, such as parents, friends, and characters on TV, who the observer may imitate. In one study, Bandura (1961) demonstrated this through the bobo doll experiment, where on seeing an adult behave aggressively towards a bobo doll, the observing child would be more likely to behave aggressively, through this observational learning. In other situations of this experiment, whether or not the child imitated the behaviour of the adult depended on whether the adult received a reward or punishment after this behaviour. This is called vicarious reinforcement.

Chapter 3

Cognitive Behavioural Therapy Similarities and Dissimilarities to Acceptance and Commitment Therapy

The History of Clinical Diagnosis

Clinical or mental health disorders have been reported throughout history. For example, in Ancient Greece, Hippocrates is generally credited for the first classification of mental illness, which included mania, melancholia, paranoia, and phobias. In his time, and without any rigorous evidence based practice, he attributed the cause of these disorders to an imbalance of the four distinct bodily fluids, known as humors, which were thought to affect temperament and health. This humeral theory was the dominant theory for mental health disorders throughout Europe until the advent of modern medical research in the nineteenth century.

In the 19th century, the humeral theory was abandoned in favor of the anatomical-clinical approach where the focus was to identify the particular psychological faculty involved in a particular form of insanity. One of these approaches was phrenology, and involved the measurement of the skull, based on the idea that the brain was the organ of the mind and that it had several localized and specific modules such as areas for morality or love.

Although today, phrenology is regarded as a pseudoscience, or obsolete primitive neuroanatomy, it had been influential in developing today's psychiatry and modern neuroanatomy (Fodor, 1983; Simpson, 2005). In 1808, a German physician coined the term ‘psychiatry’, and later, in the second half of that century, Karl Kahlbaum and Ewald Hecker developed a descriptive categorization of syndromes and Wilhelm Griesinger, at the same time developed a unitary scheme based on the concept of brain pathology. In the late 19th century, Koch referred to ‘psychotic inferiority’ to describe moral insanity, and in the 20th century this became known as ‘psychopathy’ relating to anti-social behaviour, which is still, today, recognized in the modern diagnosis for mental health disorders.

Today, the American Psychiatric Association publishes its standard criteria for the classification of mental disorders, starting in 1952 with the advent of the Diagnostic and Statistical Manual (DSM-1) to today with the newest edition, the DSM-5. The DSM-5, today, organizes each psychiatric diagnosis into five dimensions (or axis). The first axis refers to all psychological disorders except mental retardation and personality disorder, which includes depression, anxiety disorders, bipolar disorder, ADHD, autism spectrum disorders, anorexia nervosa, bulimia nervosa, and schizophrenia. The second axis refers to personality and mental retardation, which include personality disorders: paranoid personality disorder, schizoid personality disorder, schizotypal personality disorder, borderline personality disorder, antisocial personality disorder, narcissistic personality disorder, histrionic personality disorder, avoidant personality disorder, dependent personality disorder, obsessive-compulsive personality disorder and intellectual disabilities. The third refers to acute medical conditions and physical disorders, which include brain injuries and other medical disorders, which may aggravate existing mental disease. The fourth refers to psychosocial and environmental factors contributing to the disorder. The last refers to an assessment specific to children under the age of 18.

THE HISTORY OF CLINICAL TREATMENT

How mental health disorders are diagnosed, and how mental health disorders are treated has evolved through history. In ancient Greece, as they believed in the humors theory, blood clotting was believed to be caused by bad temperament and health; the treatment was mainly to let the patient (bleed), to release the clotting.

This was the dominant form of treatment throughout Europe until the 19th century, when an evidence based medical science began to emerge. In the 19th century, two major pathways of evidence based treatment for mental health disorders emerged; one based on physiology and the other based on psychology. From physiology, pharmaceuticals developed, using the psychoactive properties of plants, with Louis Lewin, in 1924, being the first to classify the drug properties of plants. One of the first discoveries of what is regarded as 'modern medicine' is where John F. Cade used lithium to treat mania, and later Paul Charpentier synthesized chlorpromazine as a neuroleptic, used to treat antipsychotic disorders such as schizophrenia. Today there are drug therapy treatments for a wide range of mental illness such as depression, schizophrenia, ADHD, anxiety disorders, bipolar disorder, etc. These, however, have been criticized for only treating the symptoms and not the causes of the disorder, and they can have powerful side effects such as memory loss, fatigue, and dependency. There are also other examples of physiological treatment for mental health disorders such as electroconvulsive therapy, where seizures are electrically induced to provide relief from mental illness, and psychosurgery, where parts of the brain are surgically destroyed in the hope that this will reduce the mental illness. However, electroconvulsive therapy and psychosurgery are extreme measures and highly controversial since, in some cases, the effects of the treatment are not reversible. Today, Cognitive Behavioural Therapy (CBT) is the dominant clinical treatment for mental health disorders.

A First Attempt at Integrating Behavioural and Cognitive Psychology; Cognitive Behavioural Therapy (CBT), the Second Wave of Behaviourism

For the psychology pathway, one of the common ways to treat depression, anxiety, eating disorders, substance misuse, etc., today, is through Cognitive Behavioural Therapy (CBT). Cognitive Behavioural Therapy is a goal-orientated therapy used to change maladaptive behaviour in an attempt to alter effects (such as depression and anxiety) and behaviour (Hassett et al., 2009).

CBT is a problem focused on action-orientated therapy, i.e., therapists focus on specific strategies to resolve specific problems. CBT is particularly effective in treating mood, anxiety, substance abuse, eating, and psychotic disorders (Lambert et al., 2004). It was developed through the integration of cognitive and behavioural psychology, 'cognitive behaviour modification' developed by Donald Meichenbaum in the 1970s, and 'behaviour therapy' developed by Edwards Thorndike and Rational Emotive Behavioural Therapy by Albert Ellis in the 1950s. It is used today to target maladaptive thinking (or errors of thinking) to alter affect, thinking and behaviour, and uses techniques such as exposure therapy, stress inoculation therapy, cognitive therapy, cognitive processing therapy, relaxation training, dialectical behaviour therapy, and acceptance and commitment therapy.

Because CBT is a goal and action orientated therapy with the focus on specific problems, it sometimes utilizes the analogy of the mind like a machine or is mechanistic, with faulty components to be either changed or removed. For example, it identifies thoughts as maladaptive or harmful, such as 'I am not good enough', or 'I am too afraid to fly', and uses specific and varied techniques to either change or remove these negative and destructive thoughts. So for example, if a CBT therapist recognized that a patient had an excessive fear of spiders, then one approach may be for the therapist to obtain behavioural modification through first identifying the target or stimuli (i.e., the spiders) and then exploring ways in which to reduce the function (emotional response) that the stimuli produces. The therapist may explicitly challenge the patient's belief that spiders are harmful, which utilizes some of the rational emotive aspects of the therapy (i.e., challenging the thoughts as irrational, directly). They may also ask the patient to write down some of the advantages and disadvantages with their current maladaptive thoughts, and how they are leading to negative fear avoidance in their lives. The therapist may also utilize desensitization approaches, such as exposure therapy, by asking the patient to first look at a picture of a spider, then when they feel comfortable, to sit in a room with a real spider in a glass, and then gradually get closer. As the patient realizes there is actually nothing to fear, the fear and anxiety (the function) of the spider (the stimuli) becomes reduced, and other spiders have less of a negative impact on the person's life (transference of stimuli function).

The Rise of the Third Wave in Behaviourism; Relational Frame Theory (RFT) and Acceptance and Commitment Therapy (ACT)

Relational Frame theory (RFT) is a behavioural account of language and higher cognition (Blackledge, 2003). It differs from traditional behavioural psychology in the sense that it proposes that it is the ability to relate things (called derived relations or inference), such as in language, as being important in higher cognitive function as opposed to simple strengths of associations, which traditional behaviourists may oppose.

The focus of this theory is how language is learned, and is based on an approach called functional contextualism. In terms of therapy, this approach focuses on the context in which thoughts, emotions and behaviour occur, and practitioners attempt to manipulate variables within the context, i.e., to change the way a person thinks, feels, and behaves. As mentioned, one of the main distinguishing features of RFT over traditional behavioural psychology is that it refers to a particular type of operant conditioning, called derived relational responding.

RFT refers to both arbitrary and non-arbitrary responding, where non-arbitrary responding may be a learned label or response, and arbitrary may be something that is unassociated with a particular event, item, or behavioural response. One of the keys to the RFT theory is that relational responding can be brought under contextual control, in that relational responses are not determined by formal properties but by the additional contextual cues. In an example of this, if A is said to be similar to B then one may infer that B, thus, must be similar to A based on the contextual control of the word 'similar' created by the verbal community. The relation established in this case, is an example of an arbitrary relation, as the relation is not based on physical properties. These arbitrarily applicable responses are the foundation of what those in the RFT community call 'relational frames'.

Relational frames include three behavioural properties: mutual entailment, combinatorial entailment, and the transformation of function (Barnes, 1994; Hayes, 1991). For mutual entailment, this involves learning that A and B are similar, and then inferring that therefore B must then be similar to A. Mutually entailed relations are not always based on similarity, for instance they can be relations of 'bigger than' and 'smaller than'. For example, if A is bigger than B, then B must be smaller than A. Another property of relational framing is combinatorial entailment. This is more complex than mutual entailment and consists of three or more relations, for example, if A is bigger than B and B is bigger than C then one can infer (or derive) that C must be smaller than A without directly learning this, (which is a key principle of why this model differs from Skinner's). In RFT, inferring one relation from another is known as derived relations. The third property of a relational frame is called transformational function, where a stimulus acquires a particular behavioural function because it derives a relation from another stimulus. For example, if A is mutually entailed with B as similar, and A is a snake and produces the behavioural function of fear, then the stimuli B could also produce that behavioural function of fear. If however, A were related to B as opposite, then rather than a behavioural function of fear and avoidance, instead behavioural responses of approach would be made. Further to this, there is evidence which suggests that relational frames can be connected to other relational frames in deep and complex networks (e.g., Lipkens, 1992; Stewart, Barnes-Holmes, Hayes, & Lipkens 2001; Stewart, Barnes-Holmes, Roche, & Smeets, 2001, 2002). These networked relating relations are what the RFT community suggests is the basis of functional analysis of behavioural properties within analogical reasoning (e.g., Barnes, Hegarty, & Smeets, 1997; Lipkens, 1992; Stewart & Barnes-Holmes, 2001; Stewart et al., 2002).

Along with a foundational architecture for how people relate items to functions and then these to other relations, RFT provides an account of theory of mind. Theory of mind (Baron-Cohen, 1991), suggests that this is the ability of an individual to identify that others have beliefs, intentions, feelings and emotions, which are independent to our own. This ability was first suggested to occur in the cognitive literature, which is the ability to perspective-take and can be traced back in research to as early as Piaget (1932), who identified the acquirement of this ability as a fundamental developmental milestone of cognitive functioning. Kolberg (1976) suggested that this ability was crucial in the development of moral reasoning, and thus has been used in interventions to reduce out-group implicit and explicit prejudice in social psychology applications (e.g., Batson et al., 1997; Dovidio et al., 2004; Galinsky & Ku, 2004; Galinsky & Moskowitz, 2000; Vescio et al., 2003).

The advantage that RFT has over other theories in the social literature (such as self-other theories) is that by using the contextual behavioural approach the theory can define the context in which the perspective-taking occurs in relation to the specific target out-group (e.g., I vs. YOU relations). RFT's description (Barnes-Holmes, Barnes-Holmes, & Cullinan, 2001) of perspective-taking involves three deictic relations, which are the interpersonal; I vs. YOU, spatial; HERE vs. THERE and temporal; NOW vs. THEN. In addition to this, and through the inclusion of the other properties of relational frames already mentioned (mutual entailment, combinatorial entailment, transformation of function and relational relations) can explain a diverse and complex array of contextual situations and has much greater flexibility than other theories that try to explain this, such as the social theories of self-other. Social theories of self-other (e.g., Cadinu & Rothbart, 1996; Smith & Henry, 1996) are restricted as they do not have a flexible account of perspective-taking. In this theory, the individual perspective-taker then a self-other categorization emerges, which leads to favorable responses towards the out-group, however this has not been shown to account for some situations (where RFT can) as it is too inflexible.

RFT was created to describe the functional mechanisms of behaviour and cognition, and to provide a framework for a theory of therapy. Based on RFT, Acceptance and Commitment Therapy (ACT; Hayes, Strosahl, & Wilson, 1999) emerged, which attempts to use functional contextualism to bring greater contextual control over relational frames such as transformation of stimulus function, which brings about painful thoughts. Functional contextualism underlies RFT and ACT, in that it is used to describe a stimuli's function under a specific context. So consider a chair with a broken leg, the function 'to sit on' is no longer appropriate except as an art exhibition, or a tool to strengthen balance, coordination, etc., then it may have a use. Therefore, under a different context, the function of the object is different and can be useful under different context. In a clinical psychology approach, these rules can also apply, such as when painful thoughts and memories under a cognitively fussed (attached) and fear avoidant context can become toxic, harmful and life distorting. However, under a defused (detached), mindful and accepting context, these painful thoughts may still be painful but not as harmful or life distorting, and do not hold the individual back from living a valued life.

ACT differs from CBT in some ways and is similar in others. ACT does not define a psychological disorder such as depression or anxiety as something to be destroyed. CBT uses a cognitive mechanism approach, like a machine with lots of separate parts. So problematic thinking, such as depressive thoughts, are seen as an analogy to faulty parts of a machine, and the aim should be to repair, replay or remove these faulty parts. Mechanistic models like CBT tend to explain some negative thoughts, feelings, schemas, narratives, and memories as dysfunctional, maladaptive, and pathological and so are fundamentally problematic. So, in dealing with these, a CBT practitioner could view these problematic states, much like the broken chair, which needs to be either fixed or removed.

ACT, using functional contextualism, would explain these maladaptive thoughts and feelings differently. Firstly ACT practitioners may prefer the word 'symptom' rather than 'maladaptive', and secondly, they may not attempt to reduce or eliminate these symptoms, but instead aim to transform the context in which the client relates to her thoughts and feelings, so that the client no longer perceives these as symptoms. An analogy of this could be seeing weeds in your garden, if you cannot remove those weeds, as they keep regrowing, then you may be consumed by thoughts about how to remove them. Fear avoidance could then develop, as you fear the judgments, which others may make when they see your weeds, and you start to avoid bringing people to your home. Sticking with this analogy, a functional contextual twist would be to view the weeds as good, or neither good nor bad, just present. For example, if someone later told you that the weeds were actually rare indigenous flowers, then the way in which you perceive them and relate with them may change in a positive way. Similarly, an ACT therapist may try to change the way in which you perceive and relate with the weeds of the mind, the maladaptive thoughts can be reduced in their impact on the patient by changing the context in which the patient relates to them. Through ACT, when a patient has negative thoughts and feelings such as 'I am not good enough', 'I am stupid', 'I am unworthy of the love and trust of others', then a practitioner may suggest that the patient uses defusion techniques such as mindfulness to detach their attention and focus away from these negative thoughts, making them less painful and less likely to cause fear avoidant behaviour, which could cascade into more painful thoughts and feelings of worthlessness. So mindfulness enables the patient to change the relationship she has with these negative feelings from one that is based in fusion and avoidance to one which is based on defusion and acceptance (i.e., being mindful). Mindfulness is seen by many ACT practitioners as the ultimate reframing tool, by moving the patient from fusion (inseparable and unhelpful focus on thoughts) and fear avoidance, to defusion (the detachment of these unhelpful thoughts) and acceptance, which are crucial for living a rich, meaningful and valued life. So, the purpose of ACT through functional contextualism is to enable mindful, valued living.

In comparison to CBT, ACT specifically tries to change negative thoughts usually through confronting and irrationalizing them. This may be similar to other aggressive methods of thought reconstruction such as thought suppression. However, thought suppression has been shown to actually increase negative thoughts, so these aggressive methods of thought reconstruction or suppression may be negative in some situations. ACT, I would argue, is also a form of thought reconstruction but through passive methods, such as defusion by the use of mindfulness. Through ACT, the thoughts are being redirected as in CBT but through passive means.

RFT, a Behavioural Theory to Debunk Chomsky?

Briefly, going back to the subject of Chomsky and behavioural psychology, many cognitive psychologists still use Chomsky to dismiss behaviourism out of hand. However, could RFT provide a reasonable account to rebuke Chomsky and all of his cognitive followers? Cognitive Behavioural models such as Relational Frame Theory, describe above, have progressed behavioural psychology to include the behavioural components of functional analysis, ABA, and then a layer of cognition in the form of inference learning, which they call derived relations. Some in this community call RFT a radical behavioural model, however, it is a Cognitive Behavioural Model because of its heavy integration with Cognitive Psychology. This integration may be a very positive step in rebuking some of Chomsky's criticisms, such as Skinner's inability to explain infinite generativity of sentences from a finite amount of words. As not all of these sentences can be directly learned though reinforcement, they must be inferred through a combination of other information learned about language, grammar, etc., to be able to generate these. RFT can account for this generativity through its accounting for inference leaning (or derived learning).

In this situation, Chomsky would only have the serious criticism of universal language rule development as a criticism of RFT's explanation for language development. It is true that RFT cannot account for why all of the cultures throughout the world (even in extremely remote places) have all developed very similar grammatical rules such as morphology, syntax, phonology, and phonetics independently from one another. If, however, the RFT model would account for aspects in information processing of the brain, which is hardwired, then Chomsky would have no criticism. It seems odd to me than many from the radical behaviourist community do not accept mental representations or information processing. Neurologists and computational neuroscientists such as Christof Koch (1998) have explained in detail and empirically validated the biophysics of computation of single and clustered (networked) neurons – hence the brain is a computational organic engine, and damage to it will effect decision making and behaviour more so than any form of reinforcement. Similarly, mental representations are our own subjective experiences and memories of the world around us, e.g., color, shape, orientation etc., so again, it seems odd to me that a behaviourist would suggest that this does not affect behaviour or even more simply, does not exist. Remembering that your car keys are left on your kitchen table relies on the memory (i.e., the mental representation, or subjective image reconstruction) of you putting your keys there and hence this mental representation effects behaviour as you choose to enter the kitchen rather than the living room to pick them up. I also find it odd that behaviourists discount hard-wired information, or behaviour without learning (which was also Chomsky's gripe). How can they possibly explain why a newborn turtle will instinctively crawl to the sea, or how a calf knows to seek milk? Do they receive reinforcement learning in the womb? Is there a behaviourist hiding in there, teaching every calf or turtle to do what they should? No, of course not, these instinctive reactions are hardwired information.

So once radical behaviourists overcome this naive perspective that everything is learned, that there is no mental representations and no hardwired information in the brain, then incorporating it into a behavioural model (such as RFT) would be an easy non-distortion of the model. In doing this, then a more full and complete model would be made, with no further serious criticism. Incorporating a hardwired language component for grammatical rules would be easily merged into a modern Cognitive Behavioural Model such as RFT, just as inference learning was, but as said, would require an adjustment in hardline radical behaviourist thinking such as ‘there is only behaviour and no information processing’ and ‘all thoughts are behaviours’. Only then could behaviourism finally be free from the haunting of Chomsky.

Chapter 4

CATEGORIZATION AND CONCEPT LEARNING: A MODERN COGNITIVE PSYCHOLOGY APPROACH

Categorization (or concept learning) is the process in which ideas and objects are recognized, differentiated, and understood (Cohen & Lefebvre, 2005). It could be argued that without the ability to learn and categorize concepts then a person would not be able to understand objects, language, and the relations between them or anything else in the world. An example of a category could be information regarding a chair, that it has a seat, legs, is used for sitting on, and is part of a larger categorical class called furniture.

There have been several theories about categorization such as classical theory, exemplar and prototypes theories, neoclassical theory, theory-theory, conceptual atomism, and essentialism. Each of these will be explained in this Chapter briefly, and the next three chapters will give special emphasis on three sub-types of exemplar theory, which are the dominant theories of categorization today (unsupervised, supervised and relational categorization).

In classical theory, which has its routes dating back to the time of Plato and Aristotle (such as in his Categories treaties), items within a category should be based on similarity to other items. More recently, Rips, 1989, argued that items should have certain critical features. Explaining concepts in terms of critical features originated with the classic view of categorization (or concept structure), such as with Katz (1972; and Komatsu, 1992). In the classic view, concepts are thought to be mentally represented as definitions and can be classified by the necessary or sufficient features. To explain this more specifically, if concept X had a necessary feature F, then in order for an instance to be classified as X, it would need to have a necessary feature F. In an example, a necessary feature of the concept 'bachelor' is to be 'male'. Without the feature 'male' then the instance cannot be classified in the category 'bachelor'. In another instance, for the concept of 'male', feature 'bachelor' is not a necessary feature for classification as not all males are bachelors. Instead, feature 'bachelor' may be a sufficient feature for classification of a male but not a necessary one.

So, in the instance of classifying a 'table', one could use the classical approach to define the necessary and sufficient features for classification. A classification of table in terms of necessary or sufficient features could be 'flat top', 'part of furniture', 'four legs', and 'used to eat on'. More recently, however, recent research has tended to be against this idea of an appropriate means for classification (Komatsu, 1992, or Murphy & Medin, 1985). In one argument against this approach, McCloskey and Glucksberg (1973) found that participants tended to disagree about the particulars in categorizing 'apple' as part of the category 'fruit', and even with themselves in subsequent trials. This suggests that category boundaries are much more fuzzy than the classical theory of sufficient and necessary features would suggest. Another problem with the definitional approach was that in most cases the definitions could not be clearly defined (Fodor, Garrett, Walker, & Parkes, 1980; Wittgenstein, 1957). In such a case, defining concepts such as 'democracy' are much more difficult and abstract than simple objects such as 'tables' or 'chairs'.

Within the classical (definition) approach, three broad streams have developed. Firstly, in light of the problems within a strict definitional approach involving 'necessary features', there is difficulty in accounting for results, which suggest that people disagree on the definitions of properties that a concept must have. This is what brought forward the sufficient vs. necessary features debate. In more recent times, a theory has been brought forward suggesting that a concept must have core defining features, which will always define the category, and it will also have non-defining features, which can lead to graded effects of categorizing (Osherson & Smith, 1981; Sutcliåe, 1993). Continuing with the idea of core features, a third branch deals with essentialism to explain categorization. In this theory, it is suggested that concepts have essential properties and are independent of people's beliefs about what constitutes a particular category (Kripke, 1972; Putnam, 1975). The problem with this approach is that there is little agreement about what a category should constitute, and no one can suggest what the essential properties of a category should look like.

Another theory about the structure of conceptual learning, called 'theory theory' suggests that it is not just perceptual similarities of features which are important for category learning, but also the general background knowledge and lay theories about the concept (Murphy & Medin, 1985). This particular theory is useful for context-based categorization, for example, why 'not coming from Mars' may be a necessary feature for the concept 'human'. This feature would not normally be considered a necessary feature for the concept 'human' but within the context of background knowledge, where 'humans' do not come from Mars, it makes sense.

In rule based approaches to classical theory, 'if' and 'then' rules are used to define a category (Smith, Patalano, & Jonides, 1998; Smith & Sloman, 1994). So, for example, if X barks then X is a dog. It is interesting to note that these If–Then rules are used in programming to assign truth and false statements (known as Boolean condition evaluates). So at a fundamental, explicit and practical level people seem to use these If–Then class assignments to understand logical expression.

In neoclassical approaches, these are extensions to classical theory, with the purpose to integrate a theory of concepts into a general theory of generative linguistics (Jackendoff, 1999). Jackendoff argues that concepts must be combinatorial and based on innate rules in order to generate an infinite number of sentences. What he means is that in order to generate many different types of sentences without direct learning for each of these then concepts are important to understand meaning and combinatorial rules are important in order to generate flexible sentences. The categorical units and structure such as thing, event, state place, property and amount are more than just bins of information, they provide a framework of relations within which generalizability, inferences, etc., can be made and lead on to the generation of infinite types of sentences. For example, the verb 'kill' is causative and indicates that one variable causes another (death in this case). A concept within the category 'path' entails a relation to a place of destination.

This theory of conceptual relations to explain the generativity of language works well with Chomsky's model for linguistics. It also bridges well with RFT, explained in Chapter 3, as both utilize conceptual relations. The main difference between the neoclassical theory and RFT is that RFT does not explicitly define mental representations and instead uses an ill-defined term, 'private event', to skirt around the need for mental representations in their model. What neoclassical theory seems to be missing is that it only recognizes innate structures and completely misses the advantages of using reinforcement learning.

Conceptual atomism is a very abstract theory of concept learning, which suggests that some concepts cannot be broken down into smaller components but can usually be built up into higher order ones. An example of this is that the concepts; 'flies', 'has wings', 'has feathers' can be combined into the concept 'bird' but individually cannot be reduced into smaller components.

Essentialism is a philosophy also used to explain concepts, where it asks the question; 'do concepts have essential qualities?' This is slightly different to the classical theory previously mentioned, as in the nature of the thought experiments given when asking this question. For example, consider the following, if a seagull called a hearing gull from Great Britain flies out and breeds with a cousin seagull species, which looks identical, is their offspring no longer a hearing gull? Necessary features from classical theory may use physical properties or abstract rules based on properties to define categorization. Essentialism may suggest that rather than certain physical properties being necessary, certain DNA or other not physical aspects are relevant in categorizing this.

Today, exemplar and prototype theories are the dominant theories of categorization and concept leaning, which is why the next three Chapters explore three distinct subtypes of these. Despite the fact that these theories are dominant, in terms of integrating behavioural psychology with the categorization theory, then aspects of most of the theories will be incorporated in the final integrative chapter.

Very briefly, before we begin a very long description into these theories, a quick description is given here for the choice of the reader to then skim over the next three chapters if they are perceived as too mathematical or explicit for this general book.

Prototype theory was created in the 1970s in response to some of the difficulties posed to classical theory. Exemplars are individual memory traces of objects or concepts whilst a prototype is an average representation of several objects or concepts. These theories only differ in the way the concept is created, i.e., a collection of all objects (exemplar theory) or an average representation (prototype theory); both of these theories are otherwise identical. Classical theory is a formal theory about the nature of the world, whereas prototype theory is a theory of an individual's relations to the world, i.e., one's prototype for a concept is dependent on her unique experiences, and not a universally necessary or sufficient feature. An example of this is that in New England most eggs are brown whilst in New York, most eggs are white, so an individual from New England would develop a prototype of an egg being brown, and New York the prototype would be white. This is a simple example of how a necessary or sufficient feature may be different from person to person and not universal as classical theory suggests, hence prototype theory somewhat extends classical theory to account for this. In the Final Chapter, 8, the prototype theory will be explained in the context of a stimuli class and combined into the behavioural model RFT as a fuller account of learning and potential rebuke to the criticisms of Chomsky.

Chapter 5

THE SIMPLICITY MODEL IN UNSUPERVISED CATEGORIZATION

Unsupervised classification deals with the problem of understanding how people organize information into categories without any prior knowledge of the items, or how they should be categorized. For example, if someone were presented with novel items, such as seeing a novel computer game or material viewed under a microscope, then the information presented might be interpreted in terms of different groups. Crucially, unsupervised categorization deals with how we group items that we have not seen before or have any idea what the items relate to.

The main technique for exploring how people organize information in an unconstrained way is through free sort tasks. In these tasks, the participant is given a collection of items and is asked, simply, to categorize these in a way that seems most intuitive. There are no feedback instructions and therefore in this case, categorization is completely intuitive. This is different to supervised categorization tasks, where constraints on categorization are included. These constraints can include feedback relating to a desired structure, general knowledge, and category. The objective in supervised categorization (e.g., Brooks, 1987; Hintzman, 1986; Medin & Schafer, 1978) is to identify the ways in which people categorize new items into existing groups, which have been already specified by the experimenter. In such a case, the experimenter attaches a label to the group, such as 'this is a group of Chomps and this is a group of Blibs', and specifies exactly which items belong to the groups. So, the main difference between these types of categorization is that one uses constraints and the other does not.

Despite this difference, unsupervised and supervised categorizations are not completely different. One shared feature of supervised and unsupervised classification is that they both make their predictions of classification (mostly) on the basis on physical similarity. More specifically, in supervised classification, the classification decisions are typically made on the basis that the new item is most similar to the items within an existing group (see Nosofsky; 1984, 1986, 1991). For example, if one category consists of triangles and another consists of squares, and then a new item is introduced, which appears more like a triangle than a square, and then participants are more likely to categorize the new item into the category that consists of triangles than the category that consists of squares. Likewise, in the unsupervised categorization, where, for example, free sort classification tasks are used, the participant has to sort items into groups using the similarity of the individual items, such as the length and width of the items. So, the key feature that both of these types of categorization share, is that they both make their predictions on the basis of physical similarity.

Unsupervised categorization can be conducted under different experimental conditions (e.g., Zippel, 1969; Imai & Garner, 1965) where, rather than predicting spontaneous categorization, the objective is to understand what factors influence categorization performance (e.g., different instructions or stimuli). An example of this is given when investigating whether the structure of the stimuli is made up of integral or separable dimensions and how the number of dimensions used in a task affects classification performance (see for example Handel & Preusser, 1970; Smith & Baron, 1981; Wills & McLaren, 1998). One example of how performance is affected by different conditions, relates to comparing the simultaneous presentation of stimuli vs. a sequential presentation. In simultaneous presentation, the spontaneous classifications between participants are similar, but in sequential presentations, the spontaneous classifications are dependent on the particular sequence of stimulus presentation (Handel and Preusser, 1969). In another example, when the stimuli were composed of separable dimensions, classification was based on a single dimension, but in contrast to this, when integral dimensions were used; classification was based on overall similarity (Handel and Imai, 1972). In a more recent case, Regehr and Brooks (1995; see also Medin, Wattenmaker, & Hampton, 1987a) suggested that a single dimension was most frequently used in classification when the constraint of asking participants to classify items into two groups was imposed, rather than having no constraints, such as in typical free sort tasks. However, in Pothos and Close (2008), it is argued that uni-dimensional sorting is not a general constraint; rather it is an artifact of the particular task employed by Ragehr and Brooks (1995). In another example, which uses a more unconstrained method, Compton and Logan (1999) used an arrangement of dots, and examined if the proximity between elements acted as a factor in determining classification results.

The previous research considered above has typically tried to identify manipulations that influence spontaneous categorization performance rather than to actually predict the classification groupings (the Compton and Logan studies are an exception to this). The simplicity model (Pothos & Chater, 2002), Rational model (Anderson, 1991) and SUSTAIN (Love, Medin, Gureckis, 2004) are three examples of unsupervised categorization models that make predictions on how the classification groupings are made.

As both the research traditions of supervised and unsupervised categorization have complementary explanatory objectives, it is useful to identify the similarities and differences between them.

SUPERVISED VS. UNSUPERVISED CATEGORIZATION

Supervised and unsupervised categorizations have some similar and some very different aspects. In exemplar models (Hintzman, 1986; Medin & Schaffer, 1978; Nosofsky, 1986), the classification of new items is made based on computing the similarity of this with each training exemplar stored in memory. In an example of how the exemplar model works, if test items are more similar to items in categories 'A' compared to items in categories 'B' or 'C' then classification of the test items into category 'A' will be made.

There are definitional accounts of categorization (e.g., Bruner, Goodman, & Austin, 1956; Katz, 1972; Katz & Fodor, 1963, Pothos & Hahn, 2000), which suggest that categories are characterized by necessary and sufficient features. In exemplar theories, (e.g., Brooks, 1987; Hintzman, 1986; Medin & Schafer, 1978), a set of known instances represent the concept, where the assignment of a new instance to a category is made on the basis of similarity to each member.

There is also the Prototype theory (e.g. Homa & Vosburgh, 1976; Homa, Sterling, & Trepel, 1981; Posner & Keele, 1968; Reed, 1972) where categorization is made on the same basis as the exemplar theory except that in this case the central tendency of the group (the prototype) is used rather than each individual exemplar. Also, according to general recognition theory

(Ashby & Perrin, 1988), intrinsic noise properties of perception and representation explain categorization effects.

The obvious difference between unsupervised and supervised categorization models is that in supervised categorization, there is a pre-specified group for how to categorize the training items, so that in this case the learner must infer the underlying category structure. In the case of an unsupervised task, the learner has no category structure to infer and therefore has to make a classification based on what is most natural and intuitive.

In experimental terms, participants are presented with artificial labels for the training stimuli by the experimenter in supervised categorization. The participant learns the group labels before a classification of a new item is made. In the real world, the application of supervised categorization seems relevant in many cases. For instance, a case of supervised categorization is when a child is told that a particular item is called an apple, while other items are called oranges. In order for the child to correctly classify new instances of apples and oranges, the child must infer from the category structure enough about the concepts of "apples" and "oranges". This is different to unsupervised categorization where in this situation we would spontaneously categorize objects without being told the category labels, and which items belong to which category.

It could be claimed that concepts are based upon supervised categorization mechanisms exclusively such as those involving the use of linguistic labels. The typical assumption in unsupervised categorization is that boundaries between groups are determined only after seeing enough exemplars of items within each group. However, children and adults generalize from a small number of examples when learning new words (e.g., Feldman, 1997; Tenenbaum & Xu, 2000). From this, the assumption can be made that there are prior constraints on which categories are plausible, and these constraints may be determined by unsupervised categorization learning. There are also strong commonalities between schemes of categorization between different cultures (e.g., Lopez, Atran, Coley, Medin, & Smith, 1997). Therefore, unsupervised categorization may help in the understanding of how supervised learning occurs.

A crucial difference in the two approaches is that in unsupervised categorization we deal with the problem of what makes a category naturally coherent. Category coherence deals with the question of what makes a category of birds or cups a coherent category but disallows non-sensible categories such as dolphins born on Tuesday.

THE SIMPLICITY PRINCIPLE

In 1986, Pomerantz and Kubovy formulated the simplicity principle to describe how the perceptual system sought the simplest rather than the most likely (see Helmholtz, 1962 for the likelihood principle) perceptual organizations, which were consistent with the sensory input given. There was much controversy as to whether the perceptual system was governed by the likelihood or simplicity principle (e.g., Pomerantz and Kubovy, 1986). However, Chater (1996) provided a mathematical account, which linked the simplicity and likelihood principles in perceptual organization using the mathematical theory of Kolmogorov complexity (e.g., Kolmogorov, 1965). This account provided evidence that the two theories were not in competition with one another, but instead were identical (at least when accounting for perceptual organization).

With the controversy partly alleviated, the simplicity principle has been applied to explain how the cognitive system imposes patterns on the world. As the world is highly patterned, the cognitive system has presumably evolved to successfully find these patterns. The simplicity principle achieves two criteria: (1) It is normatively justified; (2) It appears descriptively correct. Normative justification refers to the requirement of the principle to be consistent with theoretical arguments. In this case, evidence for this is presented in the formulation of 'Occam's razor' (William of Ockham, 1285-1349), and in early positive epistemology (e.g., Mach, 1883/ 1960), and remains a standard principle in the modern philosophy of science (e.g. Sober, 1975). In addition, over the past thirty years the theory of simplicity 'Kolmogorov complexity' has been developed and applied in mathematics (Kolmogorov, 1965), in statistics (Rissanen, 1987, 1989; Wallace & Freeman, 1987), and computer science (Quinlan & Rivest, 1989; Wallace & Boulton, 1968). This evidence gives the rigorous normative justification for the simplicity principle, which suggests that the simplest account for some data leads to the best theory for the data. Regarding (2), evidence for being descriptively correct refers to whether the theory explains specific evidence accurately. The simplicity principle in this case appears descriptively correct as demonstrated in the examples in: Mach (1959/1886), Gestalt psychology (Koffka, 1965), and in information processing research in perception (e.g., Buffart, Leeuwenberg & Restle, 1981), and in the simplicity model, Pothos & Chater (2002).

For a more thorough example of how the simplicity principle is descriptively correct, we can take the example from Gestalt psychology (Koffka, 1965). More specifically, we can consider the Gestalt law of good continuation, which states how the cognitive system completes visual patterns when part of the visual pattern is occluded.

In figure 1 (a) the vertical bar is perceived as occluding the upper left and right horizontal lines, therefore the two upper left and right horizontal lines are perceived by people as a single line as in figure 1 (b), although it could have any form as in Figure 1 (c). The simplicity principle predicts a preference for the straight line. This is because it is simpler, since there would be a shorter codelength to describe a continuation of the same pattern, as compared to altering a pattern.

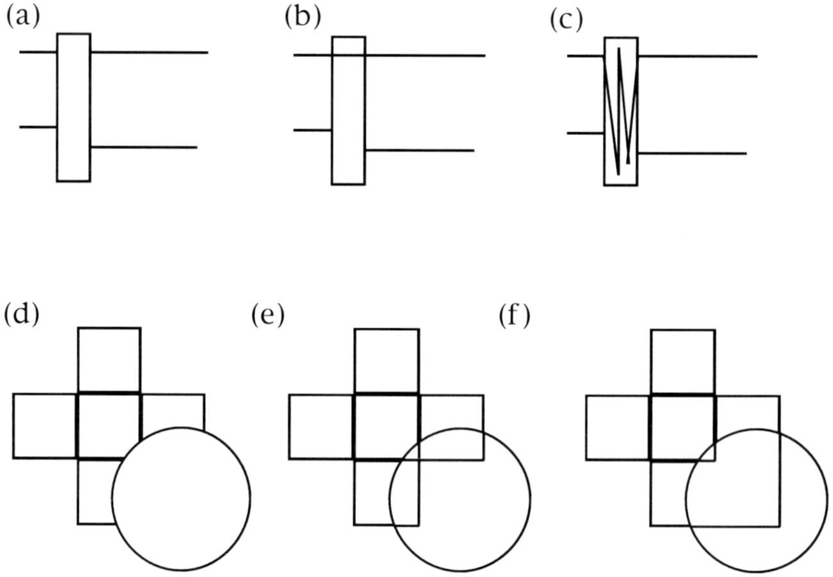

Figure 1a to f: Simplicity follows simple patterns in perceptual information processing.

When referring to the codelength of information, and the simplest codelength to describe perceived information patterns, we are referring to the measurement of information as introduced by Shannon (1948). One bit of information is the smallest piece of quantifiable information, and is a single binary decision. In categorization (e.g., Pothos and Chater, 2002), the codelength of categories are computed using the simplicity principle.

The simplicity principle is consistent with the Gestalt law of good continuation. In the case of the lower left and right horizontal lines of Figure 1 (a), this is perceived as two separate lines. This is consistent with both the simplicity principle and the Gestalt law of good continuation. In the case of the simplicity principle, the deviation of the two lower horizontal lines allows the minimal description to account for a possible disappearance of the hidden line. Therefore, the advantage of the simplicity principle is that it can postulate that the hidden line disappears. This means that the hidden line is not perceived, but can continue. When a naïve observer is presented with Figure 1 (d), this is perceived as a cross, occluded by a circle, and illustrated in Figure 1 (e). The Gestalt law of good continuation fails to account for this and leads to an interpretation of Figure 1 (f). The simplicity principle accounts for the illustration of Figure 1 (e) as this form is simpler, (it requires less codelength to describe since the deviation requires a greater codelength of description), than the more complex (greater codelength description) of the irregular Figure 1 (f).

In addition to the evidence given regarding the preference for simpler perceptual organizations, a simple mathematical illustration in favor of simplicity can be given, which supports its justification. The justification of this is given using Bayes's theorem, which states:

$$P(H \mid D) \propto P(D \mid H)P(H) \tag{1}$$

The theorem states that the probability of a hypothesis, given the data, is proportional to the product of the probability of the data given the hypothesis and the prior probability of the hypothesis without the data. The H that maximizes (1) is the same as the H that minimizes (2).

$$-\log_2 P(D \mid H) - \log_2 P(H) \tag{2}$$

Formula (2) uses Shannon's information theory for the specification of the optimal code for describing quantities such as the data, hypotheses, etc., where the optimal code minimizes the average codelength. Event x with probability $P(x)$ has the codelength $-\log_2 P(x)$. Formula (2) therefore gives the codelength for D in terms of H plus the codelength for H without D. From formulas (1) and (2) it can be seen that the most probable hypothesis is also the formula which is the simplest (i.e., is encoded with the shortest codelength). Given that both of these approaches equate to one another the general simplicity principle statement that 'when all things are equal then the simplest explanation is likely to be true can be seen as reasonable'.

MEASURING SIMPLICITY

The simplicity principle predicts that the simplest possible explanation to fit the data is often the best (Chater, 1996). When using such an approach, this could lead to the prediction that a distal scene should be uniform, however the organization must be consistent with the sensory input, and this is usually non-uniform. It is important to note that the simplicity principle predicts that the cognitive system should capture the regularities in the available information to maximize descriptive power. One question is whether the consistency with the input (capturing the regularities of the information) can be traded against the simplicity of the interpretation. Again, perceptual organization must capture the regularities in the sensory input, so the compression in the information must be compatible with the regularities in the data. If we were to ignore this point, then the simplest of explanations would be to state "anything can happen" or "group all items together as a single group", which would be completely useless as a cognitive strategy for capturing the patterns in the world. Harman (1965) suggested that the simplicity of a theory must be traded against explanatory power. However, these two factors must be stated in more specific and formalized terms in order for them to be useful as a model for category learning. The way to proceed, according to Chater (1996), is to view perceptual organization as a way of encoding information, so that the perceptual organization, which provides the simplest of encoding, is chosen. This prevents overly simple organizations that do not account for the regularities of the information to become present. This is because these encodings do not help the encoding, or the explanation of the information. Maximizing explanatory power, but also maximizing the simplicity, in encoding is both crucially desirable in accordance with the simplicity principle (the optimal state is maximum explanatory power and minimum description). If the perceptual organization fails to capture the regularities then it cannot provide a brief description of the data accurately, and is therefore useless. A useful example, which demonstrates this problem, is given in the Richard-Berry paradox (see Li & Vitanyi, 1997), which suggests there is a paradoxical problem when generating the following statement:

> "the smallest natural number that cannot be uniquely specified in less than twenty words of English" (1)

The problem here is that out of the infinite number of numbers, the smallest number N that cannot be specified in less than twenty words can be specified with the description above (1), which contains only 16 words, and hence the paradox is clear. Kolmogorov complexity avoids this problem by specifying that the description given must construct the object. Therefore, the Kolmogorov complexity of object $K(x)$ is the length of the shortest description that generates x rather than an overly general description that does not actually generate the object directly.

The measurement of simplicity has been studied extensively in philosophy, for example by Sober (1975), who suggested that no quantitative measure of simplicity has ever been universally accepted. It has also been discussed in psychology, by Attneave (1959), who suggested that the perceptual system prefers short descriptions, and been referred to as an important goal by Atick and Redlich, (1990). It is best discussed in the context of mathematics and computer science, such as in the Kolmogorov Complexity theory, which shows that identifying simplicity with brevity provides a rigorous theory of simplicity (see Kolmogorov, 1965).

Brevity of encoding can become operational using two approaches: Shannon's (1948) information theory (Attneave, 1959; Garner, 1962) and the coding theory (Simon, 1972). Structural information theory is one elaboration of this (Buffart, Leeuwenberg & Restle, 1981). We now consider the quantification of brevity.

Information Theory and Brevity

Brevity is quantified in terms of the number of bits required to distinguish the stimulus from an information source, which has a mutually exclusive range of alternatives.

The formula for this is given as:

$$I(A_i) = \log_2\left(\frac{1}{P(A_i)}\right). \qquad (1)$$

In this equation, each alternative A_i in an information source A, has the probability of occurrence $P(A_i)$. $I(A_i)$ represents the amount of information associated with the choice of a particular alternative, A_i, and is called the surprisal (surprisal can be viewed as a measure of brevity in codelength) of A_i

$$H(A) = \sum_j P(A_j) I(A_j) . \tag{2}$$

$H(A)$ is the entropy, and is the average surprisal of source A. It is the surprisal of each alternative, weighted by its probability of occurrence.

Information theory allows surprisal to be viewed as a measure of brevity. When choosing a sequence of alternatives according to the probabilities of the information source, these can be encoded in a binary sequence. The encoding gives each A_i an individual code word in the form of a sequence of binary digits (e.g. 001101). Sequences of alternatives can be concatenated into a single binary code. In accordance with the idea of brevity, the binary string that describes the alternatives is minimized as much as possible. The product of the sequence length and the average length of the code words within the sequence gives the length of the sequence code. One important implication here is that the average code of words should be minimized. If the binary string of length l_i gives the codelength for alternative A_i, then the specification for the average code word length for source A is given by:

$$\sum_j P(A_J) l_j . \tag{3}$$

There are however, some limitations of the information theory in some contexts, for example when applied to individual perceptual stimuli. An example from Leeuwenberg and Boselie (1988) involves a stimulus consisting of three letters 'aaabbbbbgg'. If we assume that there is an equal chance ($\frac{1}{3}$) of choosing one of these letters (a, b or g) then the information associated with this specification for example 'a' is $\log_2 (1/\frac{1}{3}) = \log_2 (3)$ bits of information. To specify the entire 10-letter sequence is $10 \log_2 (3)$ bits because in this case the probabilities of each item being chosen are the same for each letter.

In a different situation, where for example 'b' is chosen with probability ½ and 'a' and 'g' with probabilities ¼ then 'b's can be specified with $\log_2 (1/\frac{1}{2}) = \log_2 (2) = 1$ bit whilst the 'a's and 'g's can be specified with (1/

$\frac{1}{4}$) = $\log_2(4)$ = 2 bits, which totals 15 bits of information for the entire sequence. Having more variation in the set, such as including the entire alphabet, would lead to more information required to specify it. Information theory measures the information in the stimulus relative to the probabilities of the other stimuli. This is useful in experimental settings where the range of possibilities is limited (e.g. Garner, 1962). However, in natural perception, the range of possibilities to define the stimuli can be greater, and therefore this scheme does not provide a useful measure of brevity in encoding stimuli (Garner 1962). Another problem with the information theory is that it only states the number of bits required to specify the stimuli and not the best (most meaningful) code. It is both the nature and length of the code that is useful in understanding perceptual organization (Garner, 1974). A meaningful encoding tells us something about the actual features of the stimuli whilst a meaningless encoding randomly ascribes the code without consideration of the features.

Coding Theory and Brevity

Because of the problems with information theory, i.e., the fact that sometimes a meaningless code is ascribed to the sequences, a different approach has been sought to measure brevity, which allows featural detail to be encoded in the stimuli. The encoding of the organizations within the stimuli (i.e., the featural detail) is what Simon (1972) calls pattern languages. The shortest description of the expressed pattern language is the preferred organization. It is constrained by the number of symbols in the description (e.g., Simon, 1972) and the number of parameters (e.g., Leeuwenberg, 1969). An example of bad code would be aaabbbbbgg, which requires 10 parameters, whilst an example of good code would be 3(a)5(b)2(g), which requires just 6 parameters and hence economy is achieved. The problems with short description length is that (a) a new description language needs to be created for each perceptual stimulus, and (b) the prediction of the theory depends on the description language chosen, however Simon (1972) noted that description languages are highly correlated in their description lengths. Kolmogorov complexity generalizes coding theory and addresses these issues.

From the simplicity principle, which suggests that simple explanations that fit the data are often the best, a formulation of a much more specific simplicity model (Pothos & Chater, 2002) was proposed about how people spontaneously categorize stimuli in their environment.

THE SIMPLICITY MODEL OF UNSUPERVISED CATEGORIZATION (CATEGORY COHERENCE)

The simplicity model is designed to capture category coherence (see Figure 2 for an illustration of category coherence, i.e., greater intuitiveness) in a stimulus set (it is useful in free sort tasks of unsupervised categorization), and it assumes that there are no constraints on how the stimuli should be classified. Several theories have been suggested, which explains what constitutes category coherence. One theory is that some categories are grouped together through a common function they share (such as corkscrews having the function of opening bottles) rather than appearance, such as size, color, etc. (Barsalou, 1985). In contrast to this, other explanations suggest that categories contain items that are judged similar to each other (Quine, 1977); the simplicity model (Pothos & Chater, 2002) is one example of a model that uses similarity in classification. Murphy and Medin (1985) proposed the dominant theory of category coherence, according to which a concept is an element of people's naive theories about the world. This means that category coherence is not based on any specific piece of information, but rather on meaning in our general life. For example, regarding the concept of water, coherence is not based on its chemical structure, but rather on its meaning in our general life. For example, general knowledge could include information that tap water comes from reservoirs; it is wet and can soak our clothes, etc.

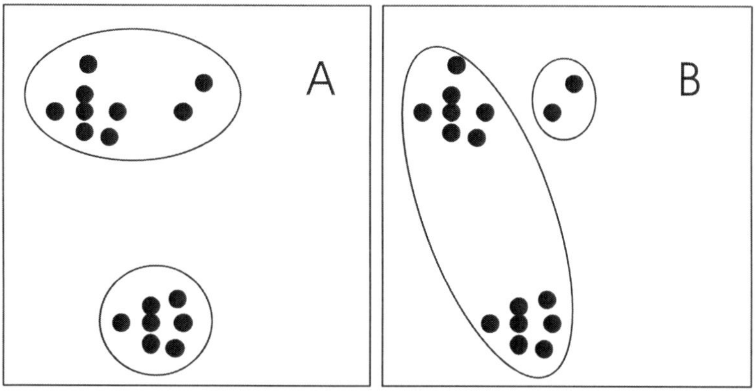

Figure 2. A simple arrangement of points in a Euclidean space. Classifications in A should be more intuitive (indicating greater category coherence) for naïve observers than classifications in B, since it involves more cohesive clusters.

Gelman and Wellman (1991), provide support for this idea by demonstrating that young children generalize on the basis of theoretical knowledge rather than physical similarity. An example of this is in the case of categorizing a worm, a person and, a toy monkey; the worm and the person were deemed more similar because both share biological properties.

The work carried out by Murphy and Medin (1985) provides compelling arguments for why a model of conceptual coherence cannot be based on similarity alone. The Simplicity model (Pothos & Chater, 2002) uses similarity information in its account of unsupervised categorization, but in principle, it could be extended to include general background information relating to particular classifications. The formalization of general knowledge has been shown to be very difficult (Dreyfus & Dreyfus, 1986; Heit, 1997). In the case of the present experimental work, stimuli that are novel and abstract are used as this avoids the problem of formalizing general knowledge.

Another aspect of categorization is that of Basic level categories, which identifies information according to a hierarchy where the classification of new items must fit the definition of a category at its 'basic level'.

Basic Level Categories and Unsupervised Categorization

Basic level categories deal with the explanation of a 'basic' level for categorization, which is a general (basic) category label in a hierarchy of categories, which can be more specific higher up the hierarchy (Rosch and Mervis, 1975). One hierarchy could include: 'Scottish highland terrier, a terrier, a dog, an animal, a living thing', etc. The default (or basic) level of categorization, for example, for a dog called 'Fido', would be that it is a dog rather than an animal or living thing. There is a wide body of evidence supporting this argument. One example of this is where basic level categories lead to more rapid picture naming, in comparison to the superordinate or subordinate categories (Rosch, Mervis, Gray, Johnson, & Boyles-Braem, 1976). There is also evidence that suggests basic level categorization is used in naming and other category related behaviourbehaviour in children (Mervis and Crisafi, 1982).

The relation between unsupervised categorization and basic level categorization can be seen if one assumes that the basic level of categorization is the category level that is most coherent, and explaining category coherence is the ultimate goal of unsupervised categorization tasks. Basic level categories have been modeled computationally (e.g., Corter & Gluck, 1992). However, basic level and unsupervised categorization do have different predictive scopes. In basic level categorization, the predictive objective is to identify the basic level category from a hierarchy of three or four category levels. There is no attempt to predict the exact way in which items are partitioned within the basic level. In unsupervised categorization, the aim is to identify the preferred classification (the classification which has the minimal descriptive length, if one adopts the simplicity model, see later) amongst all possible classifications for a particular data set.

Another important difference is that basic level categorization is based on featural representations (e.g., a dog has several known features such as a tail, a snout, paws, etc.) of objects but in unsupervised classification, the items are novel and therefore cannot be typically expressed in terms of features. In unsupervised categorization, features such as short vs. long or differences in shades of color can be used but this does not include the complex background information that is found in the basic level of categorization. Because of this, it is difficult or impossible to identify features. The advantage of the simplicity model is that it can be used to compute preferred classifications on the basis of features or independent of them whereas models for the basic level categorization are restricted to feature based categorization.

From Perception to Unsupervised Categorization

When confronted with an unfamiliar scene, the information can often be organized into different kinds of groups. This can be viewed as a process of perceptual organization, whereby sometimes we identify groups in the sensory input. It is also a process of unsupervised categorization. In order to form a mathematical model of unsupervised categorization, theoretical insights from perceptual organization can be considered, as we have done above. The two processes, 'perceptual organization' and 'unsupervised categorization', can be considered related in the sense that the perceived structure of a set of objects can lead to the (unsupervised) categorization of these items into groups.

The application of the simplicity principle to unsupervised categorization is made on the assumption that perception is based upon physical similarities (Pomerantz, 1981). Therefore, groupings made in unsupervised categorization should maximize within group similarity and minimize between group similarities. Using this assumption, we can view categorization as imposing default constraints on the similarity relations between a set of to-be-categorized stimuli.

THE SIMPLICITY MODEL OF UNSUPERVISED CLASSIFICATION

The first step in considering how the simplicity principle can be applied to grouping items into categories is to specify the data and hypotheses (a hypothesis corresponds to a possible grouping of the items). An assumption is made that the information about the similarity structure of the items corresponds to the data. The codelength required to specify the similarity structure (from standard information theory) from the objects in terms of a particular grouping is the sum of the:

> codelength to specify similarity in terms of the grouping + the codelength to specify the groupings. (1)

There is a unique codelength for each possible grouping. According to the simplicity principle (e.g., see Rissanen, 1978) there is a preference for the grouping with the shortest (most compressed) codelength. The specification of the simplicity model is made in such a way that the similarity structure with the most reduction in codelength is chosen.

The Form of the Data

In categorization research, there have been many kinds of representation assumptions. It is assumed that items can be embedded in a multi-dimensional space in spatial models of representation (e.g., Nosofsky, 1985), and that similarities are negatively monotonically related to distances in such a space. Such spatial models of representation imply an adherence to metric axioms but in some situations similarity information violates the metric axioms (Nosofsky, 1991). A representation of objects in terms of features is an alternative to this. In this case, similarity is a function of the degree to which features are shared between items, as the items correspond to bundles of features (Tversky, 1977). The problem with features is that in unsupervised classification the use of novel objects with no prior knowledge is common; it is often the case that we may not be able to express such objects in terms of features.

It is the perception of the similarity of objects that is important in the simplicity model. Similarity information can be best described in terms of internal spaces, abstract similarity relations, or features depending on circumstances. The formulation of the simplicity model is designed in a way to be compatible with different types of representation assumptions. In this way, the difficult and largely irrelevant problem of psychological representation (see Quine, 1977) is avoided. Such computational principles, which are independent of a representational assumption, have been usefully employed in other areas of cognitive science (e.g., Anderson, 1990).

The form of information that the simplicity model assumes is illustrated in the following: Consider four objects A, B, C, and D. A specification of similarity information needs to be specified, such that, for example, the similarity of 'A, B' is greater or less than the similarity 'C, D'. The formulation of the model is made in a way that similarities are never equal, and obey minimality, such that 'A, A' = 0, and symmetry, so that 'A, B' = similarity 'B, A', but they can violate transitivity. Any combination of the metric axioms can be assumed in the simplicity model and if metric axioms can be assumed for similarity relations then these can be specified with less information. Similarity is used in the implementation of the model whether symmetry and minimality is assumed or violated but there is no reason to suggest that minimality should be violated (Tversky, 1977, discusses some of the considerations that underlie some of the metric axioms). The version of the simplicity model employed in this work was implemented without the assumption of transitivity. The assumption of transitivity does not affect the computation of the codelength in the simplicity model. Transitivity is always obeyed unless the similarity information is collected with a task in which trials have the form: 'is similarity between A, B less or greater than similarity C, D?' Assuming transitivity (and all of the other metric axioms as well) is equivalent to assuming extra constraints, such as 'A, B' > 'C, D' when given 'A, B' > 'B, C' and 'B, C' > 'C, D'. The number of groups and elements in each group determine the number of extra constraints due to transitivity. The extra constraints due to transitivity will be the same where the classifications compared have similar groups, and numbers of elements in each group, so that the assumption of transitivity does not influence the optimal classification.

From information theory, it can be assumed that when deciding between two pairs A, B, and C, D, it is a binary choice to compute whether similarity (A, B) is smaller or greater than (C, D), and this is associated with one bit of information to compute. Where we have r items, we require $s(s-1)/2$ bits to specify the data directly where there are $s = r(r-1)/2$ similarities between pairs of r items and $s = r(r-1)/2$ comparisons between the similarities for pairs of items. The regularity in the specifications of the inequalities (the redundancy) means that there may be a shorter description, which captures the structure of the data. The simplicity model is one attempt to model the regularities in this structure, creating the largest saving in codelength.

Clustering by Simplicity Step 1: Coding Group

When computing the codelength required for specifying how r items are allocated into a set of n categories the allocation of all items into all possible classifications must be considered. This is given by $\sum_{v=0}^{n}(-1)^{v}((n-v)^{r}/(n-v)!v!)$ (this is Stirling's number, e.g., Graham, Knuth, & Patashnik, 1994; Feller, 1970). Using the standard information theory we can assume that $\log_2(D)$ gives us the codelength required to identify one out of D possibilities (with the assumption that each one is equally probable). Therefore, $\log_2 \sum_{v=0}^{n}(-1)^{v}((n-v)^{r}/(n-v)!v!)$ gives a codelength, which specifies the allocation of r items into groups. This, however, represents only a minor contribution to the overall computation.

In general, certain category structures are more likely to be chosen than others. For example, a category structure that consist of clusters equal to the number of items divided by two, is more likely than for example a classification where each item is in its own cluster or if all the items are clustered into a single group. The computations made in the simplicity model are based on the probability of different category structures, which are consistent with the simplicity approach. Pothos and Chater (2002) suggest that in future work, the model could identify constraints regarding the likelihood of different category structures, and this could be in the form of a non-uniform, prior probability distribution over category structures. They also suggest that general knowledge effects could be introduced here, as some groupings using general knowledge would be more plausible and therefore more likely. Such a case could include groupings based on biological vs. non-biological kinds, and thus could reduce the codelength. Where there is no general knowledge, i.e., in a case of novel items, the codelength for the classifications can be computed as above (see also Pomerantz, 1981).

Clustering by Similarity Step 2: Specifying the Data in Terms of Groups

When encoding similarity data, the definition of a cluster (or category) is that it is a collection of objects where the within cluster similarities are greater (which should be as great as possible) than the between cluster similarities (which should be as low as possible; Rosch & Mervis, 1975). Default constraints on the similarities between items are therefore introduced by a particular grouping. If the constraints are strong (i.e., many comparisons between distances are explained by them), and generally correct (i.e., there are no corrections to the constraints) then the first term in (1) is reduced.

The description of similarity inequalities that are not specified by the grouping is needed, such as between two within cluster similarities or between two between cluster similarities. If there are t of these, then the codelength will be t bits. If there are u constraints, where e are incorrect, the encoding of e must be between 0 and u, so the encoding of u requires a binary code of length $\log_2 (u+1)$ bits. Identifying the constraints e out of u constraints is done with standard combinatorics: ${}_uC_e = (u!/e!(u-e)!)$ ways to choose e items from set u. The total code for correcting erroneous constraints, E, is $\log_2(u+1) + \log_2({}_uC_e)$.

In order to specify the errors when there are very few or very many errors, a short codelength is needed. In the case of the errors, having half the number of constraints requires the greatest codelength. Pothos and Chater (2002) suggest that the number of errors should be less than half the number of constraints, and where this is not the case then no clustering should be defined, as in this case the clustering would be of dissimilar items. This additional assumption is mild, as any reasonable algorithm for finding clusters should use similarity.

The Simplicity Model, a Summary

Pairwise similarity inequalities between pairs of objects are the representation of the similarity structure in the simplicity model. The number of inequalities that must be specified is reduced with the use of categories. The disadvantage of using categories is that they require a codelength to describe the particular set of categories used and correct for any errors in the constraints. Using categories usually shortens the description of the similarity structure of the items, and the greater the simplification the more intuitive the category structure is predicted to appear. The simplicity model is evaluated in the experiments assessing naive observers' unsupervised categorization performance.

OTHER UNSUPERVISED MODELS VS. THE SIMPLICITY MODEL

Some of the early research into unsupervised learning helps illustrate the distinctiveness of the simplicity model. One of these early studies of unsupervised learning comes from Fried and Holyoak (1984), where categories are described in terms of density functions. They suggest that participants can infer the actual density function from a sample of exemplars presented to them. An assumption is needed that category distributions have a particular form (an illustration of Fried and Holyoak's theory is made with normally distributed category distributions). They also suggested that an external specification must be made of the number of categories sought. The difference between this and the simplicity model is that here we have a situation where learners know a priori that the category exemplars have properties whose range conforms to a certain distribution; another difference is that this model requires advanced knowledge of the number of categories. This corresponds to a situation where, for example, a bird expert has to identify bird categories in a new domain. The simplicity model, by contrast, does not make any assumption about the parametric properties of the categories or the number of categories sought.

AutoClass

Cheeseman and Stutz (1995) provided a model for unsupervised categorization called AutoClass, which comes from the machine learning literature. The model consists of two components, the first of which is a probability distribution, which specifies how items belong to different categories with different probabilities, as opposed to being assigned to any particular category. There is also a probability density function. This is for the distribution of the attributes of the objects that belong to the category, which constitutes the second component. Attributes can be distributed in several ways in AutoClass, as it can model many types of attribute distributions within categories and category distributions, and is not restricted to one type of probability distribution, which is unlike Fried and Holyoak's model. However, the range of probability density functions that AutoClass can employ determines the modeling scope in the AutoClass version used. This is different from the simplicity model, since a particular distribution for categories or category attributes is not assumed therefore it is more similar to Fried and Holyoak's (1984) model.

There are several related Bayesian approaches to unsupervised learning. Some of these do not use a specification on the number of categories sought. Ghahramani and Beal (2000) used a factor analysis procedure within the Bayesian framework to determine the number of factors required to model the data automatically (when considering the number of instances associated with each factor as belonging to the same cluster, then factor analysis is similar to the process of clustering). Components are rejected from the model under particular circumstances in order for this to be achieved. In contrast to the non-parametric method used in the simplicity model, Ghahramani and Beal's (2000) computations use a Gaussian function to model the distribution of information.

CODE

The CODE model by Compton and Logan (1993, 1999) is another model in which the classification of objects is guided by parametric features. It deals with the perceptual grouping of dot patterns but presumably could be used for the classification of more complex elements. In this model, a value of strength is associated with each element in a pattern that originates from the element. A group allocation is made if the patterns of strengths from the different elements at a location, when added, are above a certain threshold. As with AutoClass, the determined classifications are predicted on the basis of the strength spread. It has a parameter, which is a fixed threshold, so a single classification was predicted for a set of objects in the original formulation of CODE. The model was later adapted so that it could produce from a set of objects nested classifications (Compton and Logan, 1993, 1999).

Ahn and Medin (1992) produced a two-state model of category construction for free sort classification. The model's primary use was to evaluate the relative compellingness of a hypothesis where overall family resemblance drove the spontaneous groupings rather than sorting via a single dimension (this issue has been considered extensively in the free sort classification literature). The prediction made by this model was that there would be as many groups as there are featural values along a dimension (but there was no attempt to predict the most salient dimension).

KOHONEN NEURAL NETWORK

Schyns (1991) proposed an unsupervised model of classification. This model used a two module neural network to investigate the spontaneous discovery of categories, and the association of these categories with labels. The Kohonen neural network was used to reduce the high dimensionality input vectors to lower dimensionality (two dimensions) output vectors. This was used to find how categories were spontaneously discovered. The segregation of the output space into distinct regions can be identified with categories made by the Kohonen neural network. The similarity structure of the input distances determines the segregation into distinct regions and therefore is a spontaneous classification, rather than being determined by an external constraint. One limitation of such a model as compared to the simplicity model is that a specification of the number of categories is needed, in advance, in order to classify the information.

The Rational Model

The rational model is an incremental, Bayesian model of categorization (cf. Tenenbaum & Griffiths, 2001), and not explicitly based on similarity. It classifies a novel instance in the category, which is most likely given the feature structure of the instance (Anderson, 1991). For example, a novel

competition (regulated by a parameter). In the unsupervised learning situations considered here, if the current input item fails to activate any existing cluster above some threshold level, then a new cluster is created for the item. This is the key mechanism of 'surprise' in SUSTAIN: new clusters are created in response to surprisingly novel stimuli that do not fit with existing knowledge structures. The threshold parameter (τ) controls what level of activation is considered 'surprising' enough; so that this parameter determines the number of clusters the model creates (analogous to the coupling parameter in the rational model; Anderson, 1991).

Given that SUSTAIN is a trial-by-trial learning model, in a modeling free sorting task, where multiple items are simultaneously presented, SUSTAIN's fits are derived by running the model thousands of times on different stimulus orderings in order to create a distribution of plausible classifications: more psychologically intuitive classifications are considered to be the ones more frequently generated.

The Unsupervised GCM

The unsupervised GCM (Pothos & Bailey, 2009) is a straightforward modification in the application of the standard GCM (Nosofsky, 1991). The objective of the standard GCM is to predict the classification probabilities of new stimuli, relative to two or more pre-trained categories. For example, suppose that participants have been taught in a training phase to associate some stimuli in category A and some other stimuli in category B. Then, the GCM-predicted probability of a category A response given a new stimulus X is: $P(A|X) = \frac{\beta_A \eta_{XA}}{\beta_A \eta_{XA} + \beta_B \eta_{XB}}$, whereby $\eta_{XA} = \sum_{j\epsilon A} exp\left\{-c\left[\left(\sum_{k=1}^{D} w_k |y_{xk} - y_{jk}|^r\right)^{1/r}\right]^q\right\}$. The β terms are category biases, η_{XA} is the sum of similarities between X and all the A exemplars, c is a sensitivity parameter, r is a Minkowski distance metric parameter, q determines the shape of the similarity function, w_k are dimensional attention weights, and y's are item coordinates (it is assumed that stimuli are represented in a putative psychological space). The input to the GCM consists of the coordinates of a set of training stimuli, information about the assignment of the stimuli to categories, and the coordinates of a set of test stimuli. Behavioural data are typically fit by adjusting GCM parameters until the classification probability GCM predicts a test stimuli, X, as close as possible to the empirically observed one. An error term for the GCM can be computed as $\sum(O_i - P_i)^2$, whereby O_i are the observed probabilities and P_i are the probabilities predicted from the model.

In an unsupervised context, instead of classifying test stimuli relative to a set of training items, a consideration is made to the relative coherence of alternative partitions of a set of stimuli, where coherence means that the classification of each stimulus is predictable given the classification of the other items. Suppose we are interested in evaluating a classification for a set of stimuli, {1 2 3}{4 5 6 7 8 9} (the numbers '1', '2' etc. are stimulus ids). Each item in turn can be considered as a test item whose classification is to be predicted, and all the other items as training items whose classification is given. GCM parameters are adjusted until the predicted classification probabilities for individual 'test' items are as close as possible to 100% for the classification of interest. For example, the O_i for classifying stimulus '1' into category {2 3} would be 100%, the O_i for classifying stimulus '2' into category {1 3} would be 100%, etc. In other words, stimuli are assigned to categories in accordance with the category structure being evaluated and GCM fits are computed on this basis. Pothos and Bailey (2009) suggested that the lower the sum of all the corresponding error terms, the more coherent and intuitive a classification is predicted to be, according to the GCM.

In examining a classification, the parameters of the unsupervised GCM are automatically set in a way that the groups in the classification are as separated as possible. For example, for two-dimensional stimuli, if clusters are specified along dimension 1 but there is no classification structure along dimension 2, then optimizing the unsupervised GCM will typically produce a high attentional weight for dimension 1 and a low weight for dimension 2. In other words, the parameter search in the unsupervised GCM is guided by the particular classification structure examined, *not* by the need to produce specific empirical results.

The unsupervised GCM assumes that all stimuli are presented concurrently. Moreover, at present, it can only produce predictions of relative intuitiveness for particular partitions of a set of stimuli; it cannot (yet) be employed to identify the best possible classification for a set of stimuli from scratch.

DIVA

The divergent autoencoder, DIVA (Kurtz, 2007) is an account of human category learning based on the autoencoder connectionist architecture (Rogers

& McClelland, 2004). The DIVA model consists of a three-layer, feed forward neural network with a bottleneck-hidden layer that is trained auto-associatively using back propagation. The model operates by recoding the input at the hidden layer and then decoding (reconstructing the original input) in terms of a channel for each category (separate sets of weights connect the hidden layer to sets of output nodes that represent the feature reconstruction for each category). In supervised learning tasks, DIVA produces a construal of the input in terms of each possible category and the relative degree of reconstructive success determines the classification response. The model learns by applying the auto-associative error to adjust the weights only along the channel corresponding to the pre-determined correct category. Psychologically, the model assumes that an example belongs to a category to the extent that it can be reconstructed by the category. A category is a flexible representation of the statistical properties of the exemplars. For example, one category can correspond to all items that have value 1 on feature F1, or all items for which F1 and F2 are perfectly correlated, or all items such that feature F1 has value 1 unless features F2 and F3 each have value 0.

In unsupervised learning tasks, the model has no information about which stimuli belongs to which category or about the number of categories, so DIVA begins as a standard auto encoder with a single channel. DIVA performs unsupervised learning by evaluating stimuli one at a time. To simulate a spontaneous classification task with all stimuli concurrently available, DIVA is trained on blocks of all stimuli presented one at a time in a random order. DIVA evaluates each stimulus by determining the reconstructive success of all existing category channels (on the initial trial, there is only one category channel and no evaluation process). A spawning threshold is used to determine whether any of the existing categories provide a satisfactory account of the stimulus (i.e., a sufficiently low sum-squared error). This threshold is analogous to the coupling parameter in the rational model or the τ parameter of SUSTAIN, and it effectively determines the number of categories or clusters. If none of the existing categories meet the threshold, then the network architecture is altered: a new category channel is created and seeded by conducting one training trial with the current stimulus. After the evaluation of a stimulus, one self-supervised (input = target) training trial is conducted in which the error signal is applied only to the category channel with the best reconstruction of the current stimulus. Based on this learning procedure, a clustering solution arises in the form of category channels that specialize in reconstructing sets of stimuli with similar properties.

Chapter 6

SUPERVISED CATEGORIZATION AND ABSOLUTE JUDGMENT

AN INTRODUCTION

In categorization, there are several theories, which attempt to explain how people make classifications, such as unsupervised and supervised categorization (which this chapter explains). These theories hold their own unique perspective of how categories are formed. For example, some focus on rule formation, decision boundaries, prototype abstraction, and exemplar storage. The focus of the present investigation is to explore relative vs. 'absolute judgment' (or absolute-like representation). Absolute classification is a classification based on the actual physical properties of the items used. So, a judgment based upon absolute properties would be influenced by how physically similar an item is to another item. This is similar to the way that exemplar and prototype theories suggest that classification is made. This chapter explores the exemplar and prototype models for an illustration of what is meant by absolute representation (the terms representation and judgment are used interchangeably).

EXEMPLAR MODELS

Exemplar models (e.g., Medin & Schaffer, 1978; Nosofsky, 1986) assume that in categorization, a new item is categorized based on its similarity with existing exemplars (items) in memory. An alternative to this is the distributional approach, which suggests that classification of a new exemplar is based on the relative likelihood of belonging to each distribution. These two accounts make qualitatively different predictions. Consider the case of two categories, one of which has high variability and another, which has low variability. Exemplar theory will predict that a critical exemplar, which is exactly half way between the two categories, will be categorized as belonging to the category with low variability. The distributional model predicts that the critical exemplar should be classified into the high-variability category.

Despite the difference in qualitative prediction for categorization, the exemplar model has been successful in accounting for results, which have been used in support of other models such as prototype abstraction or rule induction. An example of this is prototypes, which are classified as better than exemplars. However, the exemplar theorists have shown that prototype enhancement effects are predicted well by pure exemplar models.

PROTOTYPE VS. EXEMPLAR THEORIES OF CATEGORIZATION

A major controversial issue in categorization literature has been whether categorization for new stimuli into existing categories occurs on the basis of comparing the similarity of the individual exemplars, within a group, with the new item (exemplar theory; e.g., Nosofsky, 1986), or by comparing the similarity of the average summary representation of the category with the new item (prototype theory; e.g., Reed, 1972). According to exemplar theory, a person will classify a new item as a member of a category if the new item is more similar to the items in this category as opposed to another. So, in this case, the previous exemplars within the pre-specified groups shape the way the classification of the new items is made, because, the category structure is given by the experimenter. This is different to spontaneous categorization. Spontaneous categorization is completely unconstrained, and has no existing categories, which suggest how the items should be classified.

In contrast to this, prototype theory suggests that when learning a category, the person abstracts a central tendency across all encountered instances of the category. In some cases, certain restricted types of prototype and exemplar models are equivalent. The controversy relates to which theory best describes the conceptual structure.

THE GENERALIZED CONTEXT MODEL OF SUPERVISED CATEGORIZATION

The Generalized Context Model (GCM; Nosofsky, 1986) has been used successfully to model exemplar (absolute) representation in categorization. This model generalizes the original version of the context model proposed by Medin and Shafer (1978), and integrates this with classic theories and ideas in the area of choice and similarity (Garner, 1974). The model uses multidimensional scaling (MDS) in modeling similarity. Exemplars are represented in multidimensional space, and similarity is a decreasing function of their distance in space.

The GCM assumes that the categorization of a new exemplar is determined by the similarity between that new exemplar and those stored in memory. The GCM sums the similarity of a new item with the items in each category and predicts that the new item will be classified in the category with the greatest summed similarity. For example, a new instance will be classified as belonging to category A rather than category B, if it is more similar to the A exemplars than the B exemplars. More specifically, exemplars are represented in a multidimensional space; each exemplar is stored together with its category label. In a simple, one-dimensional case, the distance between two stimuli S_i and S_j is given as:

$$d_{ij} = |x_i - x_j| \quad (1)$$

where x_i is the absolute magnitude of S_i, and x_j is the absolute magnitude of S_j. For an m-dimensional space, the weighted Minkowski power formula is used, so that the distance between stimuli S_i and S_j is given as:

$$d_{ij} = \left[\sum_m w_m \cdot |x_{im} - x_{jm}|^r \right]^{1/r} \quad (2)$$

In Equation (2), x_{im} denotes the value of exemplar i on psychological dimension m. The r value defines the distance metric of the psychological space. For example, the city block metric is defined with $r = 1$, and the Euclidean distance metric is defined with $r = 2$ (Garner, 1974; Shepard, 1964). Shown in Equation (2) are also the attention weight parameters w_m, which model the degree to which a participant attends to a particular dimension. The similarity between stimuli S_i and S_j is a function of their distance. Similarity is typically a monotonically decreasing function of distance, as in the equation below:

$$\eta_{ij} = e^{-cd_{ij}^{q}}, \tag{3}$$

In Equation (3) η_{ij} is the similarity between S_i and S_j; where q = 1 leads to an exponential function and q = 2 leads to a Gaussian function. The sensitivity parameter, *c*, determines how quickly the similarity between stimuli S_i and S_j is reduced with distance.

The probability of classifying stimulus S_i in category A, is proportional to the similarity between S_i and all the A exemplars, as in Equation (4); in that equation, the β_{A} parameters are category biases, which indicate whether there might be a prior bias to identify new items as being members of a particular category.

$$H_{iA} = \beta_A \sum_{x_j \in C_A} \eta_{ij}, \tag{4}$$

Finally, the actual probability of making a category A response given stimulus S_i, when there are two alternative categories (A and B), is given by Equation (5).

$$P(R_A | S_i) = \frac{H_{iA}}{H_{iA} + H_{iB}}, \tag{5}$$

OTHER SUPERVISED CATEGORIZATION MODELS

COVIS (Ashby et al., 1998)

Ashby et al. (1998) asked participants to learn to classify stimuli into two bivariate normally distributed categories. Ashby et al.'s COVIS (competition between a verbal and implicit system) model suggests there are two mental systems that compete with each other in the categorization response. It suggests, that first, there is an implicit (nonverbal) system, which learns the optimal decision boundary for separating a psychological space into regions corresponding to categories. In categorization, items above the decision boundary would fall into category A, and the items below this criterion would fall into category B. Also an explicit system learns verbal rules. The criteria set by the verbal rule are then used in categorization, so that a new item above the criterion (e.g., 10 cm) would be categorized into category A, and an item below this criterion would be categorized into category B. Ashby et al. (1998) suggested that the fact that categorization results fitted the decision boundaries (criteria) as predicted by their model was evidence in support of their model.

ALCOVE (Kruschke, 1992)

A model that is closely related to the GCM is ALCOVE (Kruschke, 1992), which incorporates the principles of the GCM within a connectionist framework. The advantage of ALCOVE is that it has an explicit mechanism that can learn the attention weights on a trial-by-trial basis. The mechanism is error driven, and therefore can learn the weights that optimize performance, rather than the experimenter having to set the weights manually for each stimuli set presented in the GCM.

RULEX (Nosofsky, Palmeri & McKinley, 1994)

Results from another study, which suggest a limitation of exemplar models, were made by Nosofsky, Palmeri and McKinley (1994). They advocated the alternative rule-plus-exception (RULEX) model of classification. From this model, they suggested that categorization is made by forming simple logical rules along single dimensions, and then storing occasional exceptions to these rules. For example, if category A consists of features 1112, 1212, 1211, 1121, 2111 (1 could mean, 'it has a feature x', and 2 could mean, 'it does not have feature x') and category B consists of 1122, 2112, 2221, 2222 then the logical value 1 can be predicted as a determining factor for what should belong in category A, and logical value 2 can be predicted for category B. So, according to the model, the individual might store value 1 on dimension 1, as a test of what belongs to category A, and value 2 on dimension 1, as a test of what belongs to category B. The exceptions stored would be 2111 for category A and 1122 for category B. The learning process in RULEX is stochastic, and a key property is that different observers can form different rules from the same information. The vast arrays of different rules are the result of a probabilistic learning process described by few free parameters.

One of the advantages of the RULEX model over the GCM is that it successfully predicted a distribution-of-generalization data, which the GCM failed to predict (Nosofsky, Palmeri & McKinley, 1994). However, Nosofsky and Johansen (2000) demonstrated that a modified version of the GCM was successful at accounting for this data by allowing for individual-subject parameter variability. Also, to gain further support for the exemplar based account of the distribution-of-generalization data; the ALCOVE (Kruschke, 1992) model was applied. In the GCM version, altering particular patterns of attention weights across the five subgroups was required, but in ALCOVE, this requirement was fulfilled by the model's attention-weight learning mechanism.

ATRIUM (Erickson & Kruschke, 1998)

ATRIUM (Erickson & Kruschke, 1998) is a multiple-system categorization model that incorporates both rule and exemplar representations. Specifically, a rule module that learns to establish single-dimension decision boundaries, an exemplar module, that learns the association between exemplars and categories, and a module that links the two together, called the competitive gating mechanism. In general, the model uses the rule module in categorization, unless there is an exception to the rule in which case it prefers the exemplar module.

Erickson and Kruschke (1998) demonstrated that when using stimuli that vary along two dimensions, the ATRIUM model accounted for the categorization performance more accurately than the GCM. Nosofsky and Johansen (2000) suggest that this was because the stimuli involved numerical data, which allowed for the precise perception of the magnitude of the items. When replicated without the numerical data there was little difference in the GCM and ATRIUM model predictions.

EXEMPLAR THEORY; THE GCM AND HOW THIS RELATES TO ABSOLUTE JUDGMENT

In the present investigation a 'relative mode of categorization (or representation)', is a categorization process in which items are represented in terms of some relational property (e.g., 'small vs. large'). A relational classification is therefore based on a relational property, which is independent of the particular physical properties of individual exemplars, but rather depends on the relations between sets of exemplars (in different categories). The implied converse mode of categorization, 'absolute categorization', involves item representations, which veridically correspond to the actual physical properties of the items (e.g., 'approximately 6 cm vs. approximately 20 cm'). It is this latter kind of categorization which the GCM has been designed to capture.

To demonstrate the specific difference in the absolute and relative representations, an account is given using the GCM which models the classifications of absolute and relative properties (not designed for relative representation but we include it here for illustrative purposes) in this example. So, in this example, the GCM is applied on the basis of two representational schemes for the training and test items: one in which the items are represented in an absolute way (in terms of their actual physical magnitudes; e.g., 12mm, 15mm etc.) and another in which the items are represented in a relative way (e.g., in terms of a simple coding whereby 'smaller' items are represented with the value 1 and 'larger' items are represented with the value '5'). For this example, all the other details of GCM fits were standard.

So, consider the following example. In the absolute version of the GCM fit, there are four items in a category called Chomps which have the heights: 32, 35, 36, 40 mm, and four items in a category called Blibs with heights: 62, 64, 66, 70 mm, and four test items, with heights: 81, 85, 121, 124 mm. It can be seen that two of the test items have 'relatively' smaller magnitudes and the other two have relatively larger magnitudes. It therefore can be asked, 'How do participants classify the test items in this experiment?' If they represented the training and test items in an absolute way, then it would be expected that most of the test items would be classified in the category of Blibs, since the Blibs training items were most similar to the test items. Using the GCM to predict the classifications made, a sum of squares value of 2.372 is produced when assigning all of the test items into the category of Blibs (note that smaller sums of squares indicate better classifications by the GCM).

Alternatively, in the relative version of the GCM fit, the relative value 1 could be used to represent all the (small) Chomps in training and the value 5 all the (large) Blib items in training. Likewise, the values 1 and 5 are used to represent the pair of smaller and larger test items respectively. Crucially, with this representational scheme, the items are only represented in terms of small and large; there is no more information about their physical (absolute) properties. As before, attempting to predict the empirical classification probabilities using the GCM and a relative representation for the training and test items, a sum of squares value of 0.181 was found for the relative classification. In other words, the GCM could predict classification probabilities better when the training and test items were represented in a relative way, as compared to when they were represented in an absolute way.

In the case of using a prototype model to represent absolute judgment, the same predictions would be made. For example, in the case of an absolute representation, the physical size of the prototypes for the 'Chomp' category and 'Blib' category would be used in the classification process. So, in the case of a pre-specified category labeled 'Chomps', which consists of heights 32, 35, 36, 40 mm, and a category labeled 'Blibs' consisting of heights 62, 64, 66, 70 mm, the prototype for the Chomp group would be 36 mm and the prototype for the Blib group would be 66 mm. In the same way as described in the GCM exemplar situation, this physical size would be used in the categorization process. So, in the case of new test items being presented corresponding to heights 81, 85, 121, 124 mm, according to prototype theory just as it was for the GCM exemplar theory, the new items would be classified with the category to which they are physically most similar. Crucially, the only difference between the prototype theory and the GCM exemplar is that in the GCM each of the individual items within a group are compared for similarity with the test items, whereas in the prototype model, it is only the abstracted prototype that is compared with the test items.

This simple example demonstrates a possible use of the GCM to account for relative properties, however, the model has been designed and adapted for the use of predicting categories in absolute modes of supervised categorization, where physical sizes of magnitudes are used.

Chapter 7

RELATIVE JUDGMENT IN CATEGORIZATION

AN INTRODUCTION

In Chapter 6, a description was given of absolute representation (or judgments) and an example was given using the generalized context model (GCM; Nosofsky; 1984). This chapter expands the literature review of absolute vs. relative representation by examining some of the literature in categorization on the subject of relative representation. Crucially, a description of the relative judgment model (RJM; Stewart et al., 2005) in categorization and analogical mapping (Gentner, 2003; Holyoak & Thagard, 1995) is given, which motivates the definition of relative representation that we will use.

ABSOLUTE IDENTIFICATION TASKS

Miller (1956) reported that the cognitive system had difficulty in processing information once the short-term capacity limit in memory was reached. He found that this limitation occurred when using many different types of information, such as loudness of tones to the magnitude of lengths and areas. Absolute identification tasks are commonly used in classification experiments when testing memory limitations. These tasks consist of presenting several items of varying size, but can be used in many other situations, such as when using sound, or brightness. In all of these situations, the participant must identify from memory, the smallest item to the largest. For example, a participant is given several stimuli of varying sizes and is asked to identify, from memory, first the smallest, then the second smallest, etc., until all the stimuli are accounted for. One of the problems that can result from this task is that errors in judgment can occur once the limit in short term memory is reached.

To be more specific, if there are too many items (i.e., if the sequence of information exceeds the capacity limits of short-term memory), the memory trace of the exemplars can be lost, which reduces identification accuracy in this task. To compensate for this loss, representation of the items in memory can shift from absolute (based on the actual physical size) to a relative representation (where the representation of the items is relative to one another. Such relative representations (e.g., see Stewart et al., 2005), utilized the relative properties of 'bigger than' or 'smaller than' the neighboring items, which is a process similar to analogical mapping. Briefly, there are three main observations in these tasks: a limit in information transmission; bow effects in the accuracy of identifying the stimuli; and sequential effects. Each of these will be explained in turn.

Limitations in Information Transmission

The amount of information that can be transmitted through short-term memory can be measured with absolute identification tasks (McGill, 1954). Information transmission has an input, the presented stimuli, and an output, the classification response made. Input information travels through the short-term memory channel and arrives as the classification response output. Perfect transmission of the input to the response, would equal perfect classifications where there would be no errors. However, Miller (1956) demonstrated that the memory channel is limited to just a few bits (2.5 bits) of information and therefore, perfect transmission, once this limit is reached, is not possible. However, as Miller (1956) points out, the memory channel is limited to just a few bits, and thus the information cannot travel perfectly from input to output if this channel capacity is exceeded. The 2.5 bit limit corresponds to about six equally likely alternatives. The limit leads to a loss of information and thus leads to a reduction in classification accuracy. Stewart et al. (2005) have demonstrated that such a limitation of memory leads to an alternative form of representation, which is based on relative properties of the items. These relative properties are based on comparisons between the item, and its preceding items, in terms of how different they are to each other. For example, the present item could be represented as 'much bigger' than the previous item. Information transmission can increase with the increase in range (e.g., the difference in size between items from smallest to largest). However, this also reaches a limit once the items are easy to discriminate (e.g., Pollack, 1952).

Bow or Edge Effects

One of the phenomena observed in absolute identification tasks is the bow effect. This is where the classification accuracy is greater at the extremes of the item set and poorer at the midrange, and hence a bow effect is observed when plotting accuracy on a graph (e.g., Kent & Lamberts, 2005). When the range of the item set increases, the classification accuracy only slightly improves. This effect is not only observed with visual stimuli such as items, it is also found with other stimuli such as when tones of sound are used (Brown et al., 2002). The bow effect increases when the number of stimuli presented increases. Siegal (1972) found that this effect was not due to any response bias, such as the end items being more frequently used compared to the midrange items.

Sequential Effects

Another observed phenomenon in absolute identification tasks is sequential effects. This is where the previous item has some influence over the perception and thus classification of the present item. For example, if the preceding item was much smaller than the current item, then the perception of the current item could be that it is smaller than it actually is. There are several theories that try to explain the sequential effect. One of these theories is the assimilation theory. In this theory, the current item is perceptually assimilated in memory by the previous item so that it is more similar to it than it actually is (Garner, 1953).

Ward and Lockhead (1970) demonstrated that a response bias led to the current item being biased away from the previous item. Evidence for the assimilation of the items has not been confined to absolute identification tasks, as this has also been shown with magnitude estimation tasks, in matching tasks and in relative intensity judgment tasks. Assimilation effects have been modeled by several researchers, including Stewart et al. (2005), in the relative judgment model (RJM).

Models That Account for the Effects Observed in Absolute Identification Tasks

Assimilation Models

Assimilation and contrast effects, (i.e., where the current item is contrasted from a neighboring item), can be accounted for by assimilation models (Holland & Lockhead, 1968). For this, it is assumed that the cognitive system generates a classification response by converging the judged distance between the current and previous stimulus. Assimilation occurs when, for example, a smaller item precedes a larger item and this results in the larger item being assimilated so that it is perceived as more similar to the previous item. Thus, the present item has been assimilated so that it is perceptually smaller than it actually is, which leads to the errors in classification judgments.

Lockhead and King (1983), provided an assimilation model, which made two assumptions: (1) that it is the successive stimuli, which are assimilated in memory, and (2) relative comparisons are made between each new item and those stored in memory from the sequence presented. The model has accounted for contrast and assimilation, because it assumes that such relative comparisons are made. However, it did not account for the information transmission limit and bow effects. Such a limitation motivated the development of other models (e.g., Stewart et al., 2005).

Modified Thurstonian Models

Thurstonian models give an account for the bow effect. The simple Thurstonian decision model has been modified many times (e.g., by Durlach and Braida, 1969). This model assumes that the items in memory are represented in a noisy way, so that the exact magnitudes are not stored in memory, but instead some unspecific representation. It is these noisy values, which are used in the classification process and this leads to the errors found in the bow effect.

The model accounts for the limit in information transmission as it assumes that the noisy values are stored instead of the exact values because of the information transmission loss from input to output. So, instead of storing the exact values of the items, the cognitive system only stores the noisy values. This accounts for why the errors in classification increase when more stimuli are presented. For example, when more items are included but the range is held constant, then the items are closer together in terms of size. As the memory representation of these are noisy, then there is a greater likelihood that these will be confused with each other, which would lead to greater errors in classification. The bow effect is accounted for by the fact that as there are less neighboring items at the extremes of the presented sets, then there is less chance of confusing these items with the neighboring items. Less confusion would lead to greater identification accuracy.

Restricted Capacity Models

Lacouture and Marley (2004) accounted for the limit in information transmission and bow effects in absolute identification tasks. They suggested that the cognitive system had a limited capacity to process information and this is why it led to the errors in the classification, such as the bow effect. The exemplars in this model are represented on a noisy Thurstonian scale. This model did well to account for the information transmission and bow effect but could not account for the sequence effects.

In more recent work, Lacouture and Marley (1995), developed a neural network-mapping model, which includes a network of one single input unit, one single hidden unit, and an output unit for each response. The storage of the exemplars in memory, were assumed noisy values. Response classifications in this model were made through the mapping onto the hidden unit activation, and it is assumed that for each output unit, activation is accumulated through the course of the trial. Once the accumulation reaches a threshold, the response is activated. However, the model still does not account for the sequence effects. Lacouture and Marley (2004) suggested that the model could be modified so that it would account for sequence effects, such as by suggesting that the normalizing of hidden activation units could be made so that previous items could be used instead of anchor values.

Laming's (1984, 1997) Relative Judgment Model

The relative judgment model (Laming, 1984), accounts for the limit in information transmission. This model gives a starting point for our definition of 'relative representation'. More specifically, the model assumes that the classifications made are done in such a way that, item differences are represented relative to each other. For example, the current item is represented relative to its difference with the preceding item.

It is clear that this model uses relative representations rather than those based solely upon absolute physical properties. For example, rather than classifying the items based upon their physical (absolute) properties, such as 'item one comes after item three because item one is 6mm and item three is 4mm', the classification is made on the basis of item one is (relatively) 'bigger than' item three. So, the representation is based on relative properties. Specifically, it is the relative difference information that is used here rather than just the relative property. This is different from the relative representation of Stewart et al. (2005) RJM, where it is the relative property 'bigger or smaller than' what is used and not the relative difference information, which is based upon the absolute properties. This model was useful to account for the limit in information transmission but failed to account for the bow and sequence effects. Laming did suggest that the model could be adapted to account for prior expectations of the distribution and thus account for these additional phenomena.

Absolute Judgment, Exemplar Models

Briefly, there are models based on similarity of absolute physical sizes. An example of how a classification would result here for three items; item one, 10mm; item two, 12mm and item three, 14mm, would be that item one would be classified with item two, rather than item three, because it is physically more similar to this, as compared to item three. There are several models, which use absolute physical similarity in classification. According to the exemplar theory, each item is stored in memory with its associated label. So, for example, when presented with a chair and the category label, chair (i.e., the participant is told that this item belongs to a category called chairs), then the item with its label 'chair', is stored in memory. When classifying a novel item, the probability of a classification is increased when the stored items and the novel items are physically more similar. So, if a chair is presented and there are two available groups, 'chairs' and 'stools', then there is a greater likelihood that the new item will be classified into the category 'chairs'. This is because its physical properties such as length, and width are more similar to the exemplars in the chair category, as compared to those in the stool group.

In terms of the absolute identification task, Brown et al. (2002) applied the data for absolute identification tasks to the exemplar model (Generalized

Context Model, Nosofsky, 1986). The exemplar model accounted for bow effects, as the end items have fewer items to get confused with, but it does not explain the gradual bowing. This however, can be accounted for if the weights in the model are changed and bias in favor of responses for stimuli that have more extreme magnitudes.

The major problem with the exemplar models is that they fail to account for sequential effects. They try to account for such effects by placing more weight to neighboring items, so that these become more available to memory. However, this fails to predict the sequence effect in classification of the items.

Stewarts Relative Judgement Model (RJM, 2005)

Stewart et al. (2005) were motivated to develop the RJM by the assumption that that the classification process in absolute identification tasks is based upon relative and not absolute judgment.

Relative vs. Absolute Judgment

The RJM assumes that when making classifications there is no mechanism, which stores even noisy perceptual absolute magnitude. Instead, the model is based on the idea that classification in absolute identification tasks are made on the basis of simple relative comparisons of the current item with its preceding neighbors. Stewart et al.'s (2005) RJM, uses a similar mapping model as used by Lacouture and Marley (2004), and assumes that there is noise in the process of mapping several stimuli to the correct output response. This noise, they suggest, is the limitation, which leads to errors in absolute identification tasks. This is different to other accounts such as the simple Thurstonian account, in that it does not require noisy representations of the perceptual exemplars. By assuming that the limit in capacity is due to mapping rather than perceptual noise, Stewart et al. (2005) suggested that there was no requirement for any further explanation to account for the lack of improvement in performance when stimulus range is increased, which makes the RJM approach more parsimonious than competing theories. One of the problems that face most models, according to Stewart et al. (2005), is that they base their assumptions on the physical magnitudes held in long-term memory, which makes it difficult to account for sequence effects. For example, in Thurstonian models, the position of criteria in long-term memory is used. In the connectionist model, Lacouture and Marley (2004), suggest that information about the most extreme stimuli is used from long-term memory. Also, in the exemplar models, the physical magnitudes of each stimulus are kept in long-term memory, and classifications are based upon similarity of these exemplars. Although these models can be modified to account for the sequence effects, the RJM explains all three observed effects in absolute identifications tasks without any need for modification.

RJM and Absolute Identification Tasks

In Stewart et al.'s (2005) relative judgment model (RJM) for absolute identification tasks, the model accounts for all three effects (bow effect, sequential effects, and limited capacity), which all the other models fail to do. The main assumption the RJM makes, which is directly relevant to the present investigation, is that the classification judgments are made on the basis of relative comparisons and not absolute magnitudes to one another. This leads to the focus of the present investigation. The question asked is whether there might be analogous situations in categorization experiments.

Relative Judgment in Analogical Mapping

Analogical mapping is a process of comparison to identify shared relations between two knowledge systems, such as two objects. The generated comparisons are thought to play a role in relational reasoning (Gentner, 1983), when learning and using rules in the appreciation of perceptual similarities, and in the production of language, science, mathematics and art. In analogical mapping when making a comparison between several objects such as elephant, truck, mouse and ball, then shared properties are identified such as elephant and truck are both 'big' and mouse and ball are both 'small'. The shared property receives a double activation and is therefore more active in the classification procedure as compared with single activated unshared properties. The shared properties can drive classification decisions: for example, because elephant and truck are both big they should be classified together, and the same happens for mouse and ball.

The Development of Relational Thought

There is evidence to suggest that the ability to reason using relational thought occurs through development (e.g., Gentner & Ratterman, 1991). Initially, children make inferences based on whole object similarity and then later acquire the ability to develop relational thought (Gentner & Rattermann, 1991). For example, consider the following situation: when given two pictures, one of which is a dog chasing a cat and another is a boy chasing a girl with the cat in the background. Three-year-old children use featural similarity to match the cat in both pictures while five-year-old children use relational similarity, e.g., in both cases chasing is taking place. This developmental trend is known as the relational shift (Genter and Rattermann, 1991).

Connectionist models based on distribution representations (e.g., Colunga & Smith, 2005) provide a good account of whole object similarity in younger children's reasoning, but do not account for more complex later relational thought. There are accounts of older childrens' and adults' reasoning ability, but these do not provide accounts of where the structured representations on which they rely originate from. There are accounts for both the featural (displayed in young children) and the relational (displayed in older children) representations, but there is no account for how the relational thought develops. This lack of an account for learning structured representations from unstructured examples is often cited as the most significant limitation of structured accounts of cognition. Doumas et al. (2008) offers an account for how structured relational thought is produced from relationally unstructured information (i.e., no direct instructions that allow for relational thought).

Analogical Mapping Modeling: DORA

Doumas et al. (2008) formed an analogical model for discovering relations (the Discovery Of Relations by Analogy; DORA). They suggested that there are three crucial factors in the development of complex learned relations. These were: firstly to identify invariants in the features presented; secondly, to isolate such property relations; and thirdly, to bind such property relations to new examples. Identifying featural invariants has been found in children as young as 6 months, who can identify features such as 'more' and 'less' in properties such as size. Doumas et al. (2008) suggested that in the next stage, the property must be isolated (such as 'taller'), from the rest of the environment, so it has its own independent meaning. The final stage is the ability to bind these property relations (e.g., 'taller'), to new items and concepts in novel situations. This takes the process from simple detection of relational properties, such as 'taller', into one, which can structure new arguments, from the same relational properties, but with novel items or concepts.

The main goal in the development of DORA was to demonstrate how an unstructured relational example could lead to structured relational representations. It forms four basic operations: (1) the retrieval of propositions from long-term memory (LTM); (2) analogical mapping of the propositions, from working-memory (WM), to the novel situation; (3) predication and refinement; and (4) self-supervised learning (SSL). Analogical mapping, inference, and schema induction, all use these four basic operations. For the purposes of the present investigation, the main interest in this literature is the binding of the relational concepts such as 'smaller than', which is relevant for the present experiments.

CONCLUSION

A relative representation is a classification based upon the relative differences of the items (e.g., bigger than, and smaller than), whilst absolute representation is based upon a classification when using the actual physical properties (e.g., item 1 is 10cm tall). Using a model like the GCM, this could be accounted for by using the actual physical sizes or abstract properties such as 'smaller than' equal to 1 and 'larger than' equal to 2. Most of the computational work seems to have focused on the physical properties (in chapter 8 these are called perceptual concepts) and not on modeling abstract properties, except for the analogical models. BehaviourBehavioural models such as RFT are thus way ahead in terms of developing a complete model of human thinking (albeit in a behaviourbehavioural context), because their learning model uses complex accounts of reinforcement contingency learning as well as inference based learning (derived relations), the vast majority of the modeling work described from the last three Chapters have focused on physical properties.

On the other hand the cognitive models described in the last three Chapters account for the crucial elements of memory limitations, which adequately account for experimental observations such as the bow effect or sequential effects, which the behaviourbehavioural model has no way of accounting for. The inability or lack of will to include mental representations and information processing in the way that Claude Shannon's information theory describes, with specific quantities of bits of information is a severe limitation for behaviourbehavioural psychology.

Chapter 8

CATEGORIES AS A STIMULI CLASS: OVERCOMING AN ONTOLOGICAL DICHOTOMY

Categories (or concepts) have been largely discussed in the cognitive literature. For example, Margolis and Laurence (1999) in their book *Concepts: Core Reading*, they include 26 articles representing the dominant theories in cognitive psychology. In reference to the behavioral perspective, they included only a footnote and ruled it out for the same arguments made against behaviorism in general (e.g., Chomsky, 1959, p6). This is the common reaction from the cognitive psychology community towards behaviorism.

In their book, a concept is defined as a subpropositional mental representation, as propositions are too big to be considered concepts. For example, in the sentence 'the chair with brocade upholstery needs to be repaired' is not a concept, it is a proposition; but 'chair' and 'upholstery' are lexical concepts – hence subpropositional. Others (e.g., Jackendoff, 1999) have argued that a concept is too difficult to define as the correctness a particular concept would have to be evaluated through, in the world view in which it plays a role, i.e., concepts, may be context dependent and have different meanings to different people. From this perspective, a concept would need to be discovered rather than given a predefinition, and is an abstract property of mental representation rather than having fixed properties.

The difficulty to define a concept can be expressed through the limitations of the major theories, which attempt to explain categorization. For example, in Chapter 6, different theories of categorization were presented. In classical theory (to define a category based on sufficient and necessary features), the limitation of this can be illustrated through an example even before the theory was first formulated.

In ancient Greece, Socrates sought to learn from Euthyphro the meaning of 'piety' and was told it is what is loved by the Gods. Socrates wondered what makes the Gods love something and asked Euthyphro to list the essential properties of the concept. Euthyphro could not and left Socrates unenlightened. This is an example illustrating the point that some concepts resist satisfactory definition in terms of anything simpler than what has already been defined.

Quine (1951) suggested that concepts are not analytic, in the sense that they can be broken down into smaller components and without any loss of the concepts meaning. Instead, Quine suggests that instead of reductionism the process is holistic. What he means by this is that statements and concepts are interconnected and that logical laws give the relation between the different statements. Therefore, it becomes impossible to draw lines between statements, which depend on experience and analytic statements, which can be broken down into components. For example, with the illustration of Socrates and Euthyphro, it is thus impossible to break down the concept of 'piety' or 'things which are loved by the Gods', with an analytic approach.

Though Quine's work was conducted several decades ago, it still has influence of some recent behavioral thinking about the nature of concepts. For example, Palmer (2002) believes, after reviewing the book *Concepts: Core Reading* and extending the work of Quine, a set of symbols is meaningless and can only be understood in relation to a network of verbal contingencies. He suggests that from this perspective the analysis of concepts is not for the logician but for the behavioral scientist. This again, however, may be an overly radical behaviorist since much of the work defined in the Chapters of categorization have demonstrated limitations with the behavioral approach of strict contingencies (systematic use of reinforcement), verbal or otherwise, as has the work of Chomsky on linguistics. So both behavioral and cognitive psychology seem for the most part to attempt to discredit the other's point of view, which as explained below is entirely unnecessary. Both behaviorism and cognitive psychology have something important to share about the development and use of concepts as well as thinking and behavior in general (which are highly concept dependent).

TYPES OF CONCEPTS OR CLASSES OF STIMULI; COGNITIVE AND BEHAVIORAL SYMMETRY

Perceptual Concepts or Perceptual Classes of Stimuli

In cognitive psychology (categorization), behaviors or decisions based on perceptual or physical features are called perpetual concepts in behavioral terms, and these are perceptual classes of stimuli, which affect behavior. These can be anything in relation to what is physically perceived, e.g., size, shape, color, movement, direction, orientation etc., and use in order to make similarity decisions. Much of the work covered in Chapters 5 and 6 on unsupervised categorization and supervised categorization are examples of perceptual categorization, which for the most part use exemplar and prototype theories to explain these.

In terms of a behavioral model a perceptual category or concept can be understood as a stimuli class, and the learning process for these are identical. In cognitive laboratory experiments, a participant is given a set of exemplars and is trained with feedback from the experimenter such as the words 'wrong' and 'correct' until they learn the category structure. In most behavioral experiments they use exactly the same procedure but call it feedback reinforcement. So, the learning of a category is the same between these two fields of psychology. Behavioral psychology also describes the function of a stimuli class, such as the same response for different types of stimuli such as the word 'cat' and the picture 'cat' evoking the same behavioral response. This too is accounted for by theories into categorization as it is not just the physical properties of an object but the associated labels which affect decision-making. In terms of physical similarity, the large bulk of categorization work has explored this in great depth and included several computational models such as those explored in Chapters 5 and 6. This work is far more developed then anything behavioral psychology has to offer. In terms of stimuli function, however, the behavioral literature seems to have defined and experimentally validated the process of function in far greater depth than cognitive psychology (categorization). So, it seems a shame that greater unity of these two fields has not been achieved. If they were, our understanding of human learning, thinking and behavior could be far more developed than it actually is today. I feel the major problem is that most behaviorists are not interested in the specifics of modeling where the resolution of understanding is great. They would rather work at a holistic level of 'all behavior' or 'generalization of reinforcement'. Similarly, some of the cognitive psychologists are more interested in the specific details of whether one computational model has a slightly better fit of data than another. Again, though this work of high resolution is important, many cognitive psychologists miss the point of holistic models such as reinforcement, contingency, learning, etc. Both of these are limited in their view and understanding of psychology. The philosopher Alan Watts alluded to this problem, in what he called the prickles and the goo, i.e., too much focus on fine detail vs. an overly general detail and without any fine detail of what is being investigated.

Associative Concepts (Stimuli Function) or Stimulus Equivalence

Associate concepts are different to perceptual concepts as they focus on stimuli within classes related in terms of shared functional properties such as those described in the work of Sideman's (1994) equivalence. Sideman (1971, 2000) refers to a stimuli equivalence class as two objects or events, which evoke the same behavioral response in a person.

In categorization, a concept that belongs to the same category can be thought of as a stimuli class as it would evoke similar behavioral responses. For example, a fork and a knife in the category of cutlery evoke the behavioral response 'to eat with', or a snake and a poisonous spider may evoke the emotional response 'fear'. Stimulus equivalence is unique as it describes the process of instantly transferring a stimulus function on a directly learned or inferred (derived) associative concept. So, for example, if a snake produced the response 'fear', and then someone told you that a snake is also called nathair, then when someone says 'there is a nathair behind you' that would evoke the same fear response as the word snake, i.e., the word nathair becomes equivalent to snake and so does its stimuli function. Associative concepts do not need to be the same in physical similarity, so as long as they evoke the same behavioral and emotional responses in individuals.

Theories of stimuli function have not been developed within cognitive psychology (categorization) to anywhere near the depth which behavioral psychology has. Broadly speaking, within categorization concepts are understood to be categorized mainly according to physical, relational or functional properties, but the development or modeling work of how function develops or operates is largely undefined. It is understood within the categorization community that chairs may be categories on the basis of shared physical properties such as having four legs and a seat or the operation of it, which is to sit on, but how this develops mechanistically is not understood in depth. This is where cognitive psychology, i.e., categorization work can benefit from the behavioral work, i.e., to understand categorical functions and how they generalize and transfer through association.

RELATIONAL CONCEPTS

The main difference between relational concepts, perceptual concepts and associative concepts is that perceptual concepts use physical properties to make similarity decisions whilst relational concepts use, quite often, abstract properties of how concepts, objects, etc., relate or differ from each other, such as object A is 'larger' than object B, where 'larger' is the relation concept. Relational categorization covers recent attempts to explain the computational model relational concept learning. This work however, such as analogical mapping, is limited in the sense that primarily explores only physical and abstract properties whilst largely ignoring functional relations (i.e., associative concepts, and stimulus equivalence).

This is another area where behavioral psychology may be ahead of cognitive psychology, in the modeling of stimuli function. Within the exemplar, prototype and analogical mapping models have been several thorough attempts to mathematically define relational concept learning, and this seems much more advanced than work within the behavioral literature. However, again, they seem to have failed to model stimuli function such as generalizability and transfer of function in any explicit model framework.

Within the behavioral model, however, RFT framework, there is overlap between the associative concepts of function transfer and relational concepts, i.e., an individual can learn the function of stimuli through inference (derived relation), rather than direct reinforcement learning.

This is another area where both areas within psychology can learn from the other. Categorization could benefit greatly from including stimuli function, and behavioral psychology would do well to include the well-defined mechanics of relational, and perceptual mental representations.

Mental Representations or Verbal Behavior?

From the evidence and arguments given in the previous Chapters, a re-examination of Chomsky's attack on behaviorism should be in order. Given the extreme view from a behaviorist that "all thoughts are behaviors" and an extreme cognitive view "all cognition is hardwired like in a computer", there can be no commonality between these two theories. However, if more moderate positions from both camps are adopted, such as "stimuli classes can be thought of like items/events in a category provoking the same behavioral responses", then great progress can be made. The criticisms of Chomsky in terms of infinite language generativity can be also dismissed as inference learning and some hardwire information can be incorporated into a model or behavioral reinforcement quite easily, as explain throughout this book, and without distorting their overall model. The apparent dichotomy between behavioral and cognitive psychology, once provided through a categorization theory perspective, can be easily dismissed and understood as two aspects of the same coin. Further efforts in these areas could easily advance both behavioral and cognitive psychology understanding of behavior and cognition and could have huge benefits in terms of future clinical models, economic behaviorism, etc.

The progress of integrating behavioral and cognitive psychology could be (and has shown to be) very far reaching. The work of integrating these at a practical and clinical level, such as with the development of CBT, has provided a model that has dominated clinical therapy for several decades. Many other area such as hierarchical learning and many other specifics about both theories have not been included in this book as the effort here was to generate a light and broad literate review of both topics rather than to consume the reader with too many new ideas. Hence, the goal here was only to provide the reader with a general overview of the commonalties between the major propositions of both behavioral and cognitive psychology rather than provide a cognitive unified behavioral model (CUB). A CUB would take many years to further empirically validate, but here at least, some of the apparent dichotomy, I hope, has been alleviated.

REFERENCES

Ahn, W. & Medin, D. L. (1992). A two-stage model of category construction. *Cognitive Science*, 16, 81-121.

Anderson, J. R. (1990). *The adaptive character of thought*. Hillsdale, NJ: Erlbaum.

Anderson, J. R. (1991). The Adaptive Nature of Human Categorization. *Psychological Review, 98*, 409-429.

Arabie, P., Hubert, L.,&de Soete, G. (Eds.) (1996). *Clustering and Classification*. River Edge, NJ:World Scientific.

Ashby, G. F., Alfonso-Reese, L. A., Turken, A. U., & Waldron, E. M. (1998). A Neuropsychological Theory of Multiple Systems in Category Learning. *Psychological Review, 105*, 442-481.

Ashby, G. F. & Perrin, N. A. (1988). Towards a Unified Theory of Similarity and Recognition, *Psychological Review*, 95, 124-150.

Atick, J. J., & Redlich, A. N. (1990). Towards a theory of early visual processing. *Neural Computation*. 2, 308-320.

Attneave, F. (1959). *Applications of information theory to psychology*. New York: Holt, Rinehart & Winston.

Bandura, A. (1977). *Social Learning Theory*. Englewood Cliffs, NJ: Prentice Hall.

Bandura, A. Ross, D., & Ross, S. A. (1961). Transmission of aggression through the imitation of aggressive models. *Journal of Abnormal and Social Psychology*, 63, 575-582.

Barnes, D., Hegarty, N., & Smeets, P. M. (1997). Relating equivalence relations to equivalence relations: A relational framing model of complex human functioning. The Analysis of Verbal Behaviour, 14, 57–83.

Barnes-Holmes, Y., Barnes-Holmes, D., & Cullinan, V. (2001). Education. In S. C. Hayes, D. Barnes-Holmes, & B. Roche, (Eds.) Relational frame theory: A post-Skinnerian account of human language and cognition. New York: Plenum.

Baron-Cohen, S. (1991). Precursors to a theory of mind: Understanding attention in others. In A. Whiten (Ed.), Natural theories of mind: Evolution, development and simulation of everyday mindreading (pp. 233-251). Oxford: Basil Blackwell.

Barnes, D. (1994). Stimulus equivalence and relational frame theory. The Psychological Record, 44, 91–124.

Barsalou, L.W. (1985). Ideals, Central Tendency and Frequency of Instantiation as Determinants of Graded Structure in Categories. *Journal of Experimental Psychology: Learning, Memory and Cognition*, 11, 629-654.

Batson, C. D., Polycarpou, M. P., Harmon-Jones, E., Imhoff, H. J., Mitchener, E. C., Bednar, L. L., et al. (1997). Empathy and attitudes: Can feeling for a member of a stigmatized group improve feelings toward the group? Journal of Personality and Social Psychology, 72, 105–118.

Blackledge, J.T. (2003). An Introduction to Relational Frame Theory: Basics and Applications. *The Behaviour Analyst Today*, 3(4), 421–34.

Brooks, L. R. (1987). Decentralized control of categorization: The role of prior processing episodes. In U. Neisser (Ed.), *Concepts in conceptual development: Ecological and intellectual factors in categorization* (pp. 141–174). Cambridge, MA: Cambridge University Press.

Brown, G. D. A., Neath, I., & Chater, N. (2002). *A ratio model of scale-invariant memory and identification.* Manuscript submitted for publication.

Bruner, J. S., Goodnow, J., & Austin, G. A. (1956). *A study of thinking*. New York: Wiley.

Buffart, H. F. J. M., Leeuwenberg, E. L. J., & Restle, F. (1981). Coding theory of visual pattern recognition. *Journal of Experimental Psychology: Human Perception and Performance*, 7, 241–274.

Cadinu, M. R., & Rothbart, M. (1996). Self-anchoring and differentiation process in the minimal group setting. Journal of Personality and Social Psychology, 70, 661-677.

Chater, N. (1996). Reconciling Simplicity and Likelihood Principles in Perceptual Organization. *Psychological Review*, 103, 566-591.

Cheeseman, P., & Stutz, J. (1995). *Bayesian classification (AutoClass): Theory and results.* In M. F. Usama, P. S.

Chomsky, N. (1959). Review of Skinner's *Verbal Behaviour. Language, 35,* 26–58.

Cohen, H., & Lefebvre, C. (Eds.). (2005). *Handbook of Categorization in Cognitive Science*. Elsevier.

Colunga, E., Smith, L. B. (2005). From the lexicon to expectations about kinds: A role for associative learning. *Psychological Review, 112,* 347–382.

Compton, B. J. & Logan, G. D. (1999). Judgments of perceptual groups: Reliability and sensitivity to stimulus transformation. *Perception Psychophysics, 61*, 1320-1335.

Compton, B. J., & Logan, G. D. (1993). Evaluating a computational model of perceptual grouping. *Perception & Psychophysics, 53*, 403–421.

Corter, J. E. & Gluck, M. A. (1992). Explaining Basic Categories: Feature Predictability and Information. *Psychological Bulletin, 2*, 291-303.

Corter, J. E. & Gluck, M. A. (1992). Explaining Basic Categories: Feature Predictability and Information. *Psychological Bulletin, 2*, 291-303.

Descartes, R; Lafleur, L. J. (translation) (1960). *Discourse on Method and Meditations*. New York: The Liberal Arts Press.

Dillenburger, K.; Keenan, M. (2009). "None of the As in ABA stand for autism: dispelling the myths". J Intellect Dev Disabil 34 (2): 193–95.

Doumas, A. A., Hummel, J. E., Sandhofer, C. M. (2008). *Psychological Review*. 115, 1, 1–43.

Dovidio, J. F., ten Vergert, M., Stewart, T. L., Gaertner, S. L., Johnson, J. D., Esses, V. M., et al. (2004). Perspective and prejudice: Antecedents and mediating mechanisms. Personality and Social Psychology Bulletin, 29, 1537–1549.

Dreyfus, H. L., & Dreyfus, S. E. (1986). *Mind over machine: The power of human intuition and expertise in the era of the computer.* New York: The Free Press.

Durlach, N. I., & Braida, L. D. (1969). Intensity perception. I. Preliminary theory of intensity resolution. *Journal of the Acoustical Society of America, 46,* 372–383.

Edwards, D. J., Pothos, E. M., & Perlman, A. (2012). Relational Vs. absolute representation in categorization. *American Journal of Psychology*. 125, 4, 481- 497.

Erickson, M. A., & Kruschke, J. K. (1998). Rules and exemplars in category learning. *Journal of Experimental Psychology: General*, 127, 107-140.

Feldman, J. (1997). The structure of perceptual categories. *Journal of Mathematical Psychology, 41*, 145–170.

Fisher, D. (1987). Knowledge acquisition *via* incremental conceptual clustering. *Machine Learning, 2*, 139–172.

Fodor, JA. (1983) *The Modularity of Mind*. MIT Press. pp. 14, 23, 131.

Fodor, J. A., Garrett, M. F., Walker, E. C., & Parkes, C. H. (1980). Against definitions. *Cognition, 18*, 263–367.

Fried, L. S., & Holyoak, K. J. (1984). Induction of category distributions: A framework for classification learning. *Journal of Experimental Psychology: Learning, Memory and Cognition, 10*, 234–257.

Galinsky, A. D., & Moskowitz, G. B. (2000). Perspective-taking: Decreasing stereotype expression, stereotype accessibility, and ingroup favoritism. *Journal of Personality*.

Galinsky, A. D., & Ku, G. (2004). The effects of perspective-taking on prejudice: The moderating role of self-evaluation. Personality and Social Psychology Bulletin, 30, 594–604.

Garner, W. R. (1953). An informational analysis of absolute judgments of loudness. *Journal of Experimental Psychology, 46,* 373–380.

Garner, W. R. (1962). *Uncertainty and structure as psychological concepts*. New York: Wiley.

Garner, W. R. (1974). *The processing of information and structure*. Potomac, MD: LEA.

Gelman, S. A., & Wellman, H. M. (1991). Insides and essences: Early understandings of the non-obvious. *Cognition, 38*, 213–244.

Gentner, D. (1983). Structure-mapping: A theoretical framework for analogy. *Cognitive Science, 7,* 155-170.

Gentner, D. (2003). Why we're so smart. In D. Gentner & S. Goldin-Meadow (Eds.), *Language in the mind: Advances in the study of language and thought* (pp. 95-235). Cambridge, MA: MIT Press.

Gentner, D., & Rattermann, M. J. (1991). Language and the career of similarity. In S. A. Gelman & J. P. Byrnes (Eds.), *Perspectives on thought and language: Interrelation in development* (pp. 225-277). London: Cambridge University Press.

Ghahramani, Z., & Beal, M. (2000). Variational inference for Bayesian mixture of factor analysers. In S. A. Solla, T. K. Leen, & K. R. Muller (Eds.), *Advances in neural information processing systems* (Vol. 12, pp. 449–455). Cambridge, MA: MIT Press.

Gureckis, T.M. and Love, B.C. (2003). Towards a Unified Account of Supervised and Unsupervised Learning. *Journal of Experimental and Theoretical Artificial Intelligence,* 15, 1-24.

Handel, S., & Imai, S. (1972). The free classification of analyzable and unanalyzable stimuli. *Perception & Psychophysics, 12*, 108–116.

Handel, S., & Preusser, D. (1970). The free classification of hierarchically and categorically related stimuli. *Journal of Verbal Learning and Verbal Behaviour*, *9*, 222–231.

Harmon, G. (1965). The inference to the best explanation. *Philosophical Review*. 74, 88-95.

Hayes, S. C., Barnes-Holmes, D., & Roche, B. (2001). Relational frame theory: A post-Skinnerian account of human language and cognition. New York: Plenum.

Hayes, S. C. (1991). A relational control theory of stimulus equivalence. In L. J. Hayes & P. N. Chase (Eds.), Dialogues on verbal behaviour (pp. 19–40). Reno, NV: Context Press.

Heit, E. (1997). Knowledge and Concept Learning. In K. Lamberts & D. Shanks (Eds.), *Knowledge, Concepts*, and Categories (pp. 7-41). London: Psychology Press.

Hintzman, D. L. (1986). Schema-abstraction in a multiple-trace memory model. *Psychological Review*, *93*, 411–428.

Holland, M. K., & Lockhead, G. R. (1968). Sequential effects in absolute judgments of loudness. *Perception & Psychophysics, 3,* 409–414.

Holyoak, K. J., & Thagard, P. (1995). *Mental leaps: Analogy in creative thought*. Cambridge, MA: MIT Press.

Homa, D., & Vosburgh, R. (1976). Category breadth and the abstraction of prototypical information. *Journal of Experimental Psychology: Human Learning and Memory, 2*, 322-330.

Homa, D., Sterling, S., & Trepel, L. (1981). Limitations of exemplar-based generalization and the abstraction of categorical information. *Journal of Experimental Psychology: Human Learning and Memory*, *7*, 418–439.

Imai, S.,&Garner,W. R. (1965). Discriminability and preference for attributes in free and constrained classification. *Journal of Experimental Psychology*, *69*, 596–608.

Jackendoff, R. (1999). What is a concept, that a person may grasp it? In E. Margolis & S. Laurence (Eds.), *Concepts: Core readings* (pp. 305–333). Cambridge, MA:MIT Press. (original work published 1989)

Katz, J. (1972). *Semantic theory*. New York: Harper & Row.

Katz, J., & Fodor, J. A. (1963). The structure of a semantic theory. *Language*, *39*, 170–210.

Kent, C., & Lamberts, L. (2005). An exemplar account of the bow and set-size effects in absolute identification. *Journal of Experimental Psychology: Learning, Memory, and Cognition, 31,* 289–305.

Koffka, K. (1965) *Principles of Gestalt psychology*. New York: Harcourt, Brace & World. (Original work published 1935).

Kohlberg, L. (1976). Moral stages and moralization: The cognitive developmental approach. In T. Lickona (E,d.), Moral development and behaviour (pp. 31-53). New York: Holt, Rinehart & Winston.

Kolmogorov, A. N. (1965). Three approaches to the quantitative definition of information. *Problems of Information and Transmission*, 1,1,1-7.

Komatsu, L. K. (1992). Recent views of conceptual structure. *Psychological Bulletin*, *112*, 500–526.

Koch, C (1998). *Biophysics of Computation: Information Processing in Single Neurons*. New York: Oxford Univ. Press.

Kripke, S. A. (1972). *Naming and necessity*. Cambridge, MA: Harvard University Press.

Kruschke, J. K. (1992). ALCOVE: An exemplar-based connectionist model of category learning. *Psychological Review*, 99, 22-44.

Kurtz, K. J. (2007). The divergent autoencoder (DIVA) model of category learning. *Psychonomic Bulletin & Review, 14*, 560-576.

Lacouture, Y., & Marley, A. A. J. (1995). A mapping model of bow effects in absolute identification. *Journal of Mathematical Psychology, 39,* 383–395.

Lacouture, Y., & Marley, A. A. J. (2004). Choice and response time processes in the identification and categorization of unidimensional stimuli. *Perception & Psychophysics, 66,* 1206–1226.

Lambert MJ, Bergin AE, Garfield SL (2004). "Introduction and Historical Overview". In Lambert MJ. Bergin and Garfield's Handbook of Psychotherapy and Behaviour Change (5th ed.). New York: John Wiley & Sons. pp. 3–15.

Laming, D. R. J. (1984). The relativity of "absolute" judgements. *British Journal of Mathematical and Statistical Psychology, 37,* 152–183.

Laming, D. R. J. (1997). *The measurement of sensation.* London: Oxford University Press.

Leeuwenberg, E. (1969). Quantitative specification of information in sequential patterns. *Psychological Review*, *76*, 216–220.

Lipkens, G. (1992). Analogical reasoning as arbitrarily applicable relational responding. Unpublished doctoral dissertation, University of Nevada, Reno.

Lockhead, G. R., & King, M. C. (1983). A memory model of sequential effects in scaling tasks. *Journal of Experimental Psychology: Human Perception and Performance, 9,* 461–473.

López, A., Atran, S., Coley, J. D., Medin, D. L., & Smith, E. E. (1997). The tree of life: Universal and cultural features of folk biological taxonomies and inductions. *Cognitive Psychology, 32*, 251–295.

Love, B. C., Medin, D. L., & Gureckis, T. M. (2004). SUSTAIN: A network model of category learning. *Psychological Review, 111*, 309-332.

Mach, E. (1959/1906). *The analysis of sensations and the relation of the physical to the psychical.* New York: Dover Publications.

Margolis, E., & Laurence, S. (1999). *Concepts: Core readings.* Cambridge, MA: MIT Press.

Maurice, C., Green, G., & Luce, S. C. (1996). *Behaviour interventions for young children with autism.* Austin, TX: Pro Ed.

McCloskey, M. E., & Glucksberg, S. (1978). Natural categories: Well-defined or fuzzy sets. *Memory and Cognition, 6*, 462–472.

McGill, W. J. (1954). Multivariate information transmission. *Psychometrika, 19,* 97–116.

Medin, D. L., & Schaffer, M. M. (1978). Context theory of classification learning. *Psychological Review, 85*, 207–238.

Medin, D. L., Wattenmaker, W. D., & Hampton, S. E. (1987a). Family resemblance, conceptual cohesiveness, and category construction. *Cognitive Psychology, 19*, 242–279.

Mervis, C. B., & Crisafi, M. A. (1982). Order of acquisition of subordinate-, basic-, and superordinate-level categories. *Child Development, 53*, 258–266.

Michalski, R., & Stepp, R. E. (1983). Automated construction of classifications: Conceptual clustering versus numerical taxonomy. *IEEE Transactions on Pattern Analysis and Machine Intelligence, PAMI-5*, 396–410. 342 *E.M. Pothos, N. Chater /Cognitive Science 26 (2002)* 303–343.

Miller, G. A. (1956). The magical number seven, plus or minus two: Some limits on our capacity for information processing. *Psychological Review, 63,* 81–97.

Murphy, G. L., & Medin, D. L. (1985). The role of theories in conceptual coherence. *Psychological Review, 92*, 289–316.

Neisser, U. (1967). *Cognitive psychology.* Appleton-Century-Crofts New York Nosofsky, R. M. (1984). Choice, similarity, and the context theory of classification. *Journal of Experimental Psychology: Learning, Memory, & Cognition, 10*, 104-114.

Nosofsky, R. M. (1985). Overall similarity and the identification of separable-dimension stimuli: A choice model analysis. *Journal of Experimental Psychology: Perception and Psychophysics*, *38*, 415–432.

Nosofsky, R. M. (1986). Attention, similarity, and the identification categorization relationship. *Journal of Experimental Psychology: General 115,* 39–57.

Nosofsky, R. M. (1991). Tests of an exemplar model for relating perceptual classification and recognition memory. *Journal of Experimental Psychology: Human Perception & Performance*, *17*, 3-27.

Nosofsky, R. M., & Johansen, M. K. (2000) Exemplar-based accounts of "multiple-system" phenomena in perceptual categorization. *Psychonomic Bulletin & Review* 7 ,3, 375-402.

Nosofsky, R. M., Palmeri, T. J., & McKinley, S. C. (1994). Rule-plus exception model of classification learning. *Psychological Review*,101, 53-79.

Osherson, D., & Smith, E. E. (1997). On typicality and vagueness. *Cognition, 64*, 189–206.

Palmer, D. C. (2002). Psychological essentialism: A review of E. Margolis and S. Laurence (EDS.). *Journal of the Experimental Analysis of Behaviour*, 78, 597–607.

Piaget, J. (1932). *The moral judgment of the child.* London: Kegan, Paul, Trench & Trubner.

Pavlov, I. P. (1927/1960). *Conditional Reflexes.* New York: Dover Publications (the 1960 edition is not an unaltered republication of the 1927 translation by Oxford University Press.

Pollack, I. (1952). The information of elementary auditory displays. *Journal of the Acoustical Society of America, 24,* 745–749.

Pomerantz, J. R. (1981). Perceptual organization in information processing. In M. Kubovy & J. R. Pomerantz (Eds.), *Perceptual organization* (pp. 141–180). Hillsdale, NJ: Erlbaum.

Pomerantz, J. R., & Kubovy, M. (1986). Theoretical approaches to perceptual organization: Simplicity and likelihood principles. In K. R. Boff, L. Kaufman, & J. P. Thomas (Eds.), *Handbook of perception and human performance, volume II: Cognitive processes and performance* (pp. 1–45). New York: Wiley.

Posner, M. I.,& Keele, S.W. (1968a). Retention of abstract ideas. *Journal of Experimental Psychology*, *83*, 304–308.

Pothos, E. M. & Bailey, T. M. (2009). Predicting category intuitiveness with the rational model, the simplicity model, and the Generalized Context

Model. *Journal of Experimental Psychology: Learning, Memory, and Cognition*.

Pothos, E. M. & Chater, N. (2002). A Simplicity Principle in Unsupervised Human Categorization. *Cognitive Science, 26*, 303-343.

Pothos, E. M. & Close, J. (2008). One or two dimensions in spontaneous classification: A simplicity approach. *Cognition, 107*, 581-602.

Pothos, E. M., & Hahn, U. (2000). So concepts aren't definitions, but do they have necessary or sufficient features? *British Journal of Psychology*, *91*, 439–450.

Putnam, H. (1975). *Mind, language and reality: Philosophical papers* (Vol. 2). Cambridge: Cambridge University Press.

Quine, W. V. O. (1951). Two dogmas of empiricism. *The Philosophical Review* 60, 20-43.

Quine,W. V. O. (1977). Natural kinds. In S. P. Schwartz (Ed.), *Naming, necessity, and natural kinds* (pp. 155–175). Ithaca, NY: Cornell University Press.

Quinlan, R. J., & Rivest, R. L. (1989). Inferring decision trees using the Minimum Description Length Principle. *Information and Computation*, *80*, 227–248.

Reed, S. K. (1972). Pattern recognition and categorization. *Cognitive Psychology*, *3*, 382–407.

Regehr, G., & Brooks, L. R. (1995). Category organization in free classification: The organizing effect of an array of stimuli. *Journal of Experimental Psychology: Learning, Memory and Cognition*, *21*, 347–363.

Rips, L. J. (1989). Similarity, typicality and categorization. In S. Vosniadou & A. Ortony (Eds.), *Similarity and analogical reasoning* (pp. 21–59). Cambridge: Cambridge University Press. Saeed, J. I. (1997). *Semantics*. Oxford : Blackwell.

Rissanen, J. (1978). Modeling by shortest data description. *Automatica*, *14*, 465–471.

Rissanen, J. (1987). Stochastic complexity. *Journal of the Royal Statistical Society, Series B*, *49*, 223–239.

Rissanen, J. (1989). *Stochastic complexity and statistical inquiry*. Singapore: World Scientific.

Rosch, E., & Mervis, B. C. (1975). Family resemblances: Studies in the internal structure of categories. *Cognitive Psychology*, *7*, 573–605.

Rosch, E., Mervis, C. B., Gray, W., Johnson, D., & Boyles-Brian, P. (1976). Basic objects in natural categories. *Cognitive Psychology*, *8*, 382–439.

Schyns, P. G. (1991). A modular neural network model of concept acquisition. *Cognitive Science*, *15*, 461–508.

Shannon, C. E. (1948). The mathematical theory of communication. *Bell System Technical Journal*. 27, 379-423, 623-656.

Skinner, B. F. (1948). Superstition' in the pigeon. *Journal of Experimental Psychology*, 38, 168-172.

Skinner, Burrhus Frederick (1957). *Verbal Behaviour*. Acton, MA: Copley Publishing Group.

Sidman, M. (1971). Reading and auditory-visual equivalences. *Journal of Speech and Hearing Research, 14,* 5–13.

Sidman, M. (1994). *Equivalence relations and behaviour: A research story*. Boston: Authors Cooperative.

Sidman, M. (2000). Equivalence relations and the reinforcement contingency. *Journal of the Experimental Analysis of Behaviour, 74,* 127–146.

Siegel, W. (1972). Memory effects in the method of absolute judgment. *Journal of Experimental Psychology, 94,* 121–131.

Simon, H. A. (1972). Complexity and the representation of patterned sequences of symbols. *Psychological Review*. 79, 369-382.

Simpson, D. (2005) "Phrenology and the Neurosciences: Contributions of F. J. Gall and J. G. Spurzheim" *ANZ Journal of Surgery*. Oxford. Vol. 75.6; p. 475.

Smith, D. J., & Baron, J. (1981). Individual differences in the classification of stimuli by dimensions. *Journal of Experimental Psychology: Human Perception and Performance*, *7*, 1132–1145.

Smith, E. E., & Sloman, S. A. (1994). Similarity- vs. rule-based categorization. *Memory and Cognition*, *22*, 377–386.

Smith, E. E., Patalano, A. L., & Jonides, J. (1998). Alternative strategies of categorization. *Cognition*, *65*, 167–196.

Sober, E. (1975) *Simplicity*, Oxford University Press.

Stewart, I., & Barnes-Holmes, D. (2001). Understanding metaphor: A relational frame perspective. *The Behaviour Analyst*, 24, 191–199.

Stewart, I., Barnes-Holmes, D., Hayes, S. C., & Lipkens, R. (2001). Relations among relations: Analogies, metaphors and stories. In S. C. Hayes, D. Barnes-Holmes, & B. Roche (Eds.), *Relational frame theory: A post-Skinnerian account of human language and cognition* (pp. 73– 86). New York: Plenum.

Stewart, I., Barnes-Holmes, D., Roche, B., & Smeets, P. M. (2001). Generating derived relational networks via the abstraction of common physical properties: A possible model of analogical reasoning. *The Psychological Record*, 51, 381–408.

Stewart, I., Barnes-Holmes, D., Roche, B., & Smeets, P. M. (2002). A functional-analytic model of analogy: A relational frame analysis. *Journal of the Experimental Analysis of Behaviour*, 78, 275–396.

Stewart, N., Brown, G. D. A., & Chater, N. (2005). Absolute identification by relative judgment. *Psychological Review*, 112, 881-911.

Sutcliåe, J. P. (1993). Concept, class and category in the tradition of Aristotle. In I. Mechelen, J. A. Hampton, R. S. Michalski, & P. Theuns (Eds.), *Categories and concepts: Theoretical views and inductive data analysis* (pp. 35–65). London: Academic Press.

Tenenbaum, J. & Griffiths, T. L. (2001). Generalization, similarity, and Bayesian inference. *Behavioural and Brain Sciences, 24*, 629-641

Tenenbaum, J. B., & Xu, F. (2000).Word learning as Bayesian inference. *Proceedings of the 22nd annual conference of the cognitive science society* (pp. 517–522). Hillsdale, NJ: Erlbaum.

Thorndike, E. L. (1898). Animal intelligence: An experimental study of the associative processes in animals. *Psychological Monographs: General and Applied,* 2(4), i-109.

Thorndike, E. L. (1905). *The elements of psychology*. New York: A. G. Seiler.

Tversky, A. (1977). Features of similarity. *Psychological Review, 84*, 327–352.

Vescio, T. K., Sechrist, G. B., & Paolucci, M. P. (2003). Perspective taking and prejudice

reduction: The mediational role of empathy arousal and situational attributions. *European Journal of Social Psychology*, 33, 455–472.

Wallace, C. S., & Boulton, D. M. (1968). An information measure for classification. *Computing Journal, 11*, 185–195.

Wallace, C. S., & Freeman, P. R. (1987). Estimation and inference by compact coding. *Journal of the Royal Statistical Society, Series B, 49*, 240–251.

Ward, L. M., & Lockhead, G. R. (1970). Sequential effect and memory in category judgment. *Journal of Experimental Psychology, 84,* 27–34.

Whelan, R., & Barnes-Holmes, D. (2004). A derived transformation of consequential functions in accordance with the relational frames of same and opposite. *Journal of the Experimental Analysis of Behaviour*, 82, 177–195.

William of Ockham, 1967-88. *Opera philosophica et theologica*. Gedeon Gál, et al., ed. 17 vols. St. Bonaventure, N. Y.: The Franciscan Institute.

Wills, A. J., & McLaren, I. P. L. (1998). Perceptual learning and free classification. *The Quarterly Journal of Experimental Psychology*, *51B*, 235–270.

Wittgenstein, L. (1957). *Philosophical investigations* (3rd ed.). Oxford: Blackwell.

Zippel, B. (1969). Unrestricted classification behaviour and learning of imposed classifications in closed, exhaustive stimulus sets. *Journal of Experimental Psychology*, *82*, 493–498.

AUTHOR'S CONTACT INFORMATION

Dr. Darren J. Edwards,
Research Fellow,
Department of Psychology
Swansea University,
Singleton Park
Swansea SA2 8PP
Tel: 07447976690
Email: D.J.Edwards@swansea.ac.uk

INDEX

C

D